Creating Environments for Troubled Children

There are those moments
when I could again
feel as a child

Creating Environments for Troubled Children

by Douglas Powers

The University of North Carolina Press *Chapel Hill*

© 1980 The University of North Carolina Press

All rights reserved

Manufactured in the United States of America

Cloth ISBN 0-8078-1418-0

Paper ISBN 0-8078-4061-0

Library of Congress Catalog Card Number 79-19735

Library of Congress Cataloging in Publication Data
Powers, Douglas, 1920–
    Creating environments for troubled children.

    1. Child psychotherapy—Residential treatment.   2. Children—Institutional
care.   3. Psychiatric consultation. I. Title.
RJ504.5.P68   362.7'4   79-19735
ISBN 0-8078-1418-0
ISBN 0-8078-4061-0 pbk.

To my wife, Anne Elizabeth, and our children, Anne, John, and Tom, and to all my child teachers, past and yet to be, especially Bruce, the first one, who is now a grandfather

Contents

Part II. Essays on Children's Problems

Foreword

When children's homes, or orphanages, were founded, most often in the years between 1870 and 1920, there were in most communities numbers of children in need of care. There were the true orphans; many parents died during their child-rearing years. There were the children who belonged to nobody, the "little wanderers" or the "waifs and strays" for whom two early children's homes were named, one in America, one in England. There were destitute children whose parents simply could not afford to feed or clothe them. And unless these children were taken into the homes provided by many churches and some civic organizations, the alternative was the workhouse, the almshouse, or the minimal existence of the county home.

Because there were many more children in need than children's homes could provide for, these homes naturally selected the most promising, the most trainable, the better behaved. Even today some homes retain a vestige of this past in their application process, which requires the signature of a pastor testifying to the fact that this is a "worthy child." And those who were not worthy, those who rebelled, those who were ungrateful for what had been done for them—if such children had been admitted, by mistake, as it were, they were ignominiously dismissed. An old lady of my acquaintance who was reared in such a home recalls her fear and trembling when the superintendent entered the dining hall. His mission was all too often that of publicly casting out some "ungrateful" youngster whose behavior did not meet the standards expected of a child to whom such charity had been shown. She was convinced, each time the superintendent appeared, that some peccadillo of her own had been discovered and that she would be thrown to the wolves.

In the 1930s and 1940s a number of things happened that changed this picture radically. Improved medical care sharply reduced the number of orphans, although it often kept alive but not well parents who formerly would have died. Destitution, although it still existed, was taken care of, in many instances, by the government's new welfare programs, particularly Aid to Dependent Children, although here again the inadequacy of the program often kept families together but on a very low level of subsistence. County and state child welfare programs received federal subsidies under the Social Security Act. The number of needy, unattached children declined sharply. At the same time the number of children whose parents, though still living, had neglected, abused, or abandoned them increased. So did the number of so-called disturbed or problem children. But perhaps the factor that affected the children's home most was a wave of antiinstitutional feeling and a perhaps somewhat unrealistic belief in the virtues of foster family care. The new state and county agencies automatically tried to place dependent and neglected children in foster family homes. They turned to the children's home only if they could not find a foster home, or if the child's behavior was such that no foster home could keep him.

As a result, children's homes, instead of caring for promising, grateful orphans, found themselves with more and more disturbed, difficult, rebellious youngsters who saw coming to a home not as a benefit but as a punishment, as an unwarranted interference with their right to be with their own parents from whom they still demanded love, or as one more in a series of rejections. At every child-care conference the theme was the same: The children we have today are much more disturbed than those we cared for in the past. And they are becoming more so, year after year.

These disturbances are basically of three kinds. Putting aside for the moment that disturbance due to genetic or physiological factors, which perhaps we are only at the very beginning of identifying and treating, there is the disturbance that appears to be largely due to faulty relationships or perhaps to undue pressures in the child's family. There is the disturbance due to the very fact that the child is not at home: the anger, guilt, loss of self-worth, and apprehension that accompany having to leave one's parents and live elsewhere. And lastly there is the disturbance caused by unwise attempts to protect the child or to provide him with a kind of care thought to be good for him when he is in no way ready to accept it. This last kind of disturbance is definitely iatric. Among the instances Dr. Powers cites in this book, there are several that show a child bandied about from foster home to foster home, not because of any weakness in the foster homes themselves but because the child was nowhere near ready to accept substitute parents on being removed from his own.

Children's homes reacted in different ways to the increased disturbance of the youngsters referred to them, often in response to local conditions and to financial considerations. Mainly in the North, East, and West, where public foster home programs grew most rapidly, the more progressive homes completely reversed their intake policies. Instead of seeking out promising, easy-to-care-for youngsters, they set out to deal with disturbed children by design. They became what is known as residential treatment centers, caring only for children whose behavior was such that something had to be done about it. This change did not come about all at once: Dr. Powers gives a vivid description of such a home in transition, almost at the present time. Such centers are badly needed, in the South as well as the North, East, and West, but good treatment centers require spending a great deal of money on a very few children, and there are other functions for which children's homes are needed.

A children's home may serve to clarify family plans and relationships when there has been some sort of family breakdown. This is not the place to discuss the potentials of this kind of care. I have done so elsewhere.[1] But in many communities, and particularly in the South, children's homes are being used—rightfully, I would maintain—for many children whose major problem is not their own behavior but the behavior of their parents. These homes are not treatment centers by intent, nor are they equipped or organized to be so. Yet many of the children in them are confused or disturbed, for all three of the reasons discussed above, although perhaps principally for the second and third—the problem of being away from home and the damage done by repeated rejections in foster homes.

Children's homes that accept children largely because of family breakdown have had to face the problem of the disturbed child.

1. See Alan Keith-Lucas and Clifford W. Sanford, *Group Child Care as a Family Service* (Chapel Hill: University of North Carolina Press, 1977), to which Dr. Powers contributed a chapter describing the treatment of three children and one family group.

Some have tried to do so by attempting to screen out the more disturbed child at intake. In this they have not been entirely successful, especially as some forms of disturbance do not become really threatening until adolescence. Some still dismiss children for misbehavior, not as traumatically perhaps as in the orphanage days, but under the rubric of a "need for services not available at this home" or some such formula. But most have recognized that some of their children will need therapy of some kind and have sought it through either mental health centers or a consulting psychiatrist. It is no reflection on the value of such treatment to say that some homes have been so much impressed with the problems of some of the children they have in care that they have forgotten why these children came to them and have behaved as if they were residential centers without the resources necessary to do that job and to the neglect of their primary responsibility to the family group. They have also sometimes prescribed treatment for children whose problems are not in themselves.

Yet many such children do need help from a psychiatrist. And there is another group, both in the treatment center and in the family-oriented children's home, who may also need a psychiatrist's help. This is the staff, who may need help not only in meeting the needs of children but in meeting their own needs, which, in the long run, may amount to the same thing. Caring for troubled children in an institutional setting is a most wearing and difficult job, and one that may easily create or exacerbate problems in one's own relationships both within and outside the work situation. When we add to this the fact that it is largely performed by untrained, underpaid, and overworked people—a relic of the comparatively placid and uncomplicated orphanage days—mental health principles applied to staff become very important. They need not only to create a therapeutic milieu for children but to find one for themselves.

Dr. Powers has had experience both with treatment centers and with less specialized children's homes. He writes both as a participant in the life of a center or a home and as an observer— not, one is forced to say, an entirely unbiased one, for he is clearly an advocate for children and a believer in the value of certain kinds of relationships. One does not have to agree with all of his statements and speculations to recognize how helpful he can be to children.

The book falls into two parts: first, a series of essays directly related to helping in a children's home at various levels, from consultation to administration to life in a cottage to the individual treatment of a child; then, some more general essays on children's development and problems.

But Dr. Powers is more than a physician and psychiatrist. He is a poet, and a fine one. Each essay in this book is preceded by a poem, sometimes satirical in tone, sometimes illuminating, and in one instance a retelling of the essay's story in more feeling words. These poems, in my opinion, do even more than the text to carry the message of the book and to emphasize the warmth, the concern for children, and the humility that Dr. Powers brings to his work and that is so important in helping troubled children cope with the problems in their lives.

Alan Keith-Lucas
Little Switzerland, North Carolina

RECURRENCE

There are those moments
relegated to memory
as year follows year
that recur
under right conditions.

You have created
those moments for me
many times
when I could again
feel as a child
and yet know
as a man.

A Note on Consultation

It has been said that anyone who has been a child and has grown to adulthood may be considered an expert on child growth and development. Perhaps this is true to some extent. Certainly consultants about children, from diverse educational and training experiences, populate the earth. They consult on everything about children from preconception to second childhood.

Child psychiatrists are no exception; they are consultants, too. Until completion of residency training their education and experience are generally standardized. They are graduates of approved medical schools and they intern for a year after receiving the M.D. degree. They undergo residency training in both adult and child psychiatry, and five postgraduate years are required before they are eligible for certification by examination of the American Board of Psychiatry and Neurology.

Among the many important areas covered in the training phase are normal growth and development, psychopathology of children and families, neurological disorders, psychosomatic disorders, crisis coping, pediatric disorders and their concomitant emotional reactions, social and cultural factors in illness, and extensive supervised experience in the various therapy modalities, including chemotherapy. The training is designed to include outpatient, inpatient, and community experience. Throughout the training the resident takes on clinical administrative duties commensurate with developing skills and participates in group and/or individual research projects.

After completion of residency training, the child psychiatrist may focus on one or more of the many areas of child care. (The use of the word *child* is understood to include the adolescent age group as well.) Thus, a practitioner may function as a generalist, working with children (and their families) from infancy through adolescence. Or, one may work with a specific age group, for example, preschool children, school-age children, or adolescents. This work may take place in a number of settings, including offices, hospitals, school systems, mental health clinics, public health programs, community-based programs such as day-care centers and children's homes, residential treatment programs, or some combination of these.

Because of the scope and extent of their medical and psychiatric training and experience, child psychiatrists should be equipped to provide helpful consultation in a number of kinds of children's programs. The writer, for instance, has been closely identified with residential treatment programs for many years. With this focus in practice he has been used extensively as a consultant by child-caring agencies such as other residential centers, children's homes, and day-care programs.

It is important in the beginning for both consultant and agency to have as clear an understanding as possible about what kind of service the agency is seeking. Often, this cannot be clearly defined but has to develop out of the continuing relationship. Usually, requests for consultation are broad-based and generally include treatment of children and families and supervision of psychotherapy; sometimes in-service training at different levels is requested, and invariably the consultant is asked to suggest ways and means of improving the total program as he becomes familiar with the operation.

This last charge is probably the area in which conflict is most likely to occur. A consultant in many respects is like a guest in a house and must remember this. A guest may observe and even suggest changes, but he cannot directly bring about change and cannot help unless there is sanction of the suggested idea and action by the administration. Yet most directors are willing to explore ideas reasonably presented and are vitally concerned about improving their programs.

If the basic wish to improve exists in the director, the staff, and the consultant, improvement in quality of program almost always occurs. There may be many starts and stops, based on many reality factors, but the most stultifying roadblocks usually are the various myopic views of those involved. Much discussion and many compromises are necessary, but these actions clarify matters

PART I

Helping in a Children's Home

Acknowledgments

Throughout the book all names, places, and dates have been changed. Some of the case material has been altered in form, but the content is authentic. The photographs accompanying the chapters were made in a number of locations over a time period of several years. There is no case material in the book that relates to any child whose picture appears. Grateful appreciation is hereby expressed to the children, parents, and guardians who kindly gave permission for use of the photographs.

To my late dean, Dr. John Bryant Chase, Jr., and to Mr. Malcolm Call, editor-in-chief, The University of North Carolina Press, for their continuing encouragement; to Dr. Alan Keith-Lucas, for his invaluable advice on organizing and editing and for his kindness in writing the Foreword; to my colleague, Mr. Gene Bennett, who helped prepare the original material for Chapter 10, "Helping Children Find Their Past"; to Betty Cauble for her patience in deciphering my laborious longhand in the typing of the manuscript; and to colleagues, past and present, too numerous to mention.

CONSULTANTS

Consultants may not
Or they may
Be helpful
On any given day
Their pearls may fall
Albeit on deaf ears
Or their drivel
May jam on ears
Hyperacute for years
But like spreading poverty
And cheap movie houses
Consultants are omnipresent
Some loud, some quiet as mouses
They come in various colors
Short, tall, thin and stout
Some male, some female
Perhaps hermaphroditic
They blow in
Blow off
And blow
Out

that you said . . ." Difficulty also arises when a staff member feels that his good ideas are not being heard and tries to form an alliance, or coalition, with a consultant in opposition to the administration.

Children may make the psychiatrist's job harder when they feel stigmatized because they are seeing a psychiatrist. "Seeing a psychiatrist means that I am crazy." This feeling is sometimes reinforced by other fearful children and by unwitting staff members.

The administrator may ask for ideas in a number of areas, but when they are presented he has the uneasy feeling that he should have "thought of that myself." This can lead to the rejection of good ideas or to an inordinate delay while the idea becomes compatible to the administrator. Finally, there is the consultant who oversteps the bounds of the relationship and tries directly or indirectly to take over some administrative functions, with resulting resentment by administration and further confusion of staff.

These are just a few of the more obvious pitfalls in any consultant-agency relationship. Again, there are many factors and many subtleties of action, and a continual across-the-board dialogue is necessary for clarification and understanding. Some conflicts are preventable and others, if they do occur, are reversible. But it takes time and work; and above all the goal of the agency—help for troubled children and families—must be kept in plain view by everyone. If it is, therapeutic attitudes will change, and improved direct and indirect care for the children will result.

for all concerned and contribute to changes that are rationally based.

It has been said that the ideal consultant is one who plays the role of visiting expert, dresses appropriately (and usually differently from staff), and is engaged (though it is not so stated) to support the judgment of the director.

A particular consultant may serve a needed public relations function for a given agency, but one would hope that program improvement is the primary motivation of all concerned. If the "ideal" function already mentioned does in fact exist, the inert agency-consultant relationship is unlikely to sustain itself for very long.

A consultant is able to view many aspects of a program over a period of time and, by virtue of not being burdened by the day-to-day struggles inherent in any program, may be in a position to see the incongruities and discontinuities with a relatively fresh eye.

A long list of potential program problem areas could be compiled and several of these will be discussed in Chapter 1. At this time brief attention will be directed to some of the problems that may arise in the process of consultation.

In a staff that is inexperienced in using a psychiatric consultant, several attitudes often surface at once. There are those who regard the psychiatrist as the answer to all the agency's (and sometimes their own) problems; there are those who become very defensive and want no part of such "hocus-pocus"; and there are those who adopt a "maybe" or "wait-and-see" attitude. Some staff members, particularly houseparents, actually tamper with the child-therapist relationship by interrogating the child after individual sessions to find out what was talked about. They view the child-therapist relationship as a competitive one and contribute to appointments being missed through "errors" in scheduling. Sometimes they see the therapeutic relationship as an indication that the houseparent is viewed by someone as not doing an effective job.

Other staff members try to become "instant" psychiatrists themselves; they conduct long, extractive, persuasive sessions with the child or misuse general information revealed by the therapist at case conferences by talking openly about it before other children or confronting the child with such a statement as "Dr. Blank said

CHAPTER I

Creating a Therapeutic Environment

To help the child to understand,
to learn, to trust

THE CHILD FIXERS

I

Some programs for Wayward Youth
have a way it seems, like water
of seeking the lowest level
in ways quite strange
to their first conception

Now it may be a false assumption
but it generally appears
that the first well-springs
of program motivation
were fed by honest impulse

But sometimes something happens
over time out there or in here
which muddies contaminates
dries up diverts or floods
that initial motive

So that the image presented
reminds one of a dry-cleaning
emporium, heralded always
by flashing blinking Neon
"Suffer little children"

While inside the child fixers
hover over ringing tills
stirring vats of hydrocarbons
mordants waterproofing
and guaranteed repellents

Let us fix your Wayward Youth
pick-up in three hours
regular processing one week
storage in off seasons
more economical by the bagful

II

Somehow that first motive
may be lost forever
if the faculties of the fixers
become dulled in time
from the poisonous vapors
rising above the tanks
from the high-decibel whine
of promotion self-adulation
for all to hear

With permanent near vision
never seeing the larger world
the assembly line moves on
while fallacious fixers
perpetually perpetrate
themselves in words
and words in fact
become the facts

The foremost goal of any therapeutic effort is to help the child understand as much as possible about himself, the origins of his behavior, and the consequences of such behavior, but no amount of individual or group therapy can achieve this unless the child is provided with a setting where he can experiment with and find other methods of relating and other ways of behaving that will be more gratifying and productive. The ultimate goal is to help the child learn to be less destructive of himself and that part of society at large in which he will eventually live.

Neither goal is likely to be achieved in isolation. For treatment to approach success, a coordinated effort is required on the part of the entire child-caring staff. This means every professional person as well as every nonprofessional and support person. Such an ideal state of functioning rarely exists more than briefly in a child-caring institution because of the multiple factors involved, but it can be approached to the point where a very effective program can be realized. There is no alchemists' formula for reaching such a state of functioning, but it can be done. Central to its achievement is the idea that each person must become bigger than his or her craft, bigger than himself or herself, a statement that implies a relatively stable self-identity, a capacity for tolerance of overlap of work effort and territory, a clear view and reasonable acceptance of the goals of the child-caring agency, a good understanding and possession of some ever-improving skills in helping children with emotional and social problems, and an ongoing attitude of problem solving. Underlying all of this is the criterion that each person must have a healthy respect for self, which makes possible respect for one's colleagues and the children. The person who can muster a reasonable number of these qualities can perhaps live with a certain amount of uncertainty and tolerate a certain amount of hostility without becoming dysfunctional. Both of these latter abilities seem to be highly desirable for those who work with disturbed children and their families.

In such a setting there must be a strong, prevailing therapeutic attitude throughout the staff, one based on self-understanding as well as on an understanding of the dynamics and needs of any particular child. There must also be an understanding of the group needs of staff as well as children.

To create a therapeutic environment in a residential program is no easy task. It takes time. No director, board of control, consultant, staff member, or section of a program can do it alone. There are always problems to solve. One problem solved may create another. There is linkage among every individual in the program, every section in the program. No one stands alone.

In a residential program a list of potential problems would be endless, but a few key considerations in any attempt to mount an effective treatment program demand serious attention. Any program that seeks therapeutic effectiveness, its reason for being, cannot avoid dealing with these issues.

The first problem is that of personnel. The prospective professional staff member—psychiatrist, social worker, psychologist—generally gets a thorough looking-over. Vital but less recognizably professional staff (cottage counselors, houseparents, child-care workers, or whatever they are called) are often employed after one interview, perhaps with only one person. Often, they do not meet and talk with others in a similar category; references are seldom checked; and the person interviewing may have had little experience and no formal training in making such an important decision.

Many such new employees have no overall idea of the goals of the agency and cannot see where their efforts are of importance to the program. Yet this is the very place where planned orientation is needed. Each employee needs to know the "who, which, what, how, when, and where" of the total program. Some time spent in orientation in every facet of the program would be most valuable in helping employees to become allies.

Then, too, in-service training often exists only in name or not at all. Many child-care workers are hired one day and assigned to full duty the next, with no continuing in-service training and with little knowledgeable backup from a supervisor. It is not unusual for a supervisor of child care to be in that position without formal training and with only a few more months of child-care experience than those being supervised—and sometimes with less experience than those being supervised.

In this kind of situation, the anxiety of the inexperienced staff turns to confusion and anger. These emotions trigger similar ones in the children, and very soon there is an atmosphere destructive to all concerned. Child-care workers begin making individual judgments about the meaning of behavior and the appropriate kinds of management to attempt. Almost the only consistency is the prevailing inconsistency. This is a prime atmosphere for the rapid emergence of a suppressive "crime and punishment" approach, with anxiety, anger, acting-out, and mistrust at all levels.

Something has to give in this kind of environment. Incidence and intensity of combativeness among children may increase; runaways mount; children may be discharged. Individual staff members may leave in despair. When they do, administration must fill vacancies on a crash basis, and often this adds fuel to the fire. The whole nightmarish process becomes cyclical, and many events in the chain of emotional upheaval are reminiscent of the uncontrolled fury from which so many children are referred for help.

On the positive side, some strength, some reason, usually emerges from within the staff so that the disturbances subside and a semblance of normality gradually returns. But much far-reaching damage has occurred. Staff members are likely to be so relieved at the lull in battle that they do not adequately review the recent course of events in an effort to uncover and resolve basic contributing factors. They do not examine the past experience and try to learn from it.

In such circumstances poor child-care practices are likely to prevail. Some of this can be corrected if the agency provides clear general guidelines that it considers basic to good child-caring attitudes and procedures. In the absence of such guidelines, each counselor or set of cottage parents becomes relatively autonomous and will assert authority in such a way as to maintain control of children rather than help them learn. Punishments such as the following may result: frequent whipping of younger children and the administration of hard paddlings, albeit infrequently, to early- and midadolescent children; washing out the mouths of younger children with soap when they use forbidden words; restricting children (latency-age and adolescent) to their rooms for several days at a time or forcing them to sit on the steps for several hours; allowing, or sometimes subtly encouraging, one child to physically harm another with whom the child-caring person is angry; and withholding snacks for some minor infraction of the rules.

A common complaint of children and adolescents in residence is that they have little or no privacy. This is expressed in many ways, and staff needs to be sensitive to these complaints. Children complain that houseparents go through their belongings without permission. Another frequent concern of adolescent boys is the young housemother who comes into their rooms unannounced; and the converse is true with adolescent girls and male houseparents.

Children and adolescents enter child-caring institutions with varying degrees of dependency and pseudoindependence. The long-range aim from the day of admission must be in the direction of a realistic interdependence with others. Too often the institutional attitude is such that many children are inhibited in their search for relative autonomy. Too many discussions are held *about* them, too many decisions are made *for* them, often with the result that they have had very little practice at helping to manage their own lives by the time they leave the institution.

Another factor that may militate against the establishment of a therapeutic milieu is the agency's need to maintain its public image. If this is threatened, its financing and indeed very existence may be at stake. Who will fund the program, and to whom is the agency beholden for its continuance? What do the consumers of the service (those who refer children) think of the product? If the agency is strongly church related or supported by a church, what will the church authorities (particularly the board of directors) think of the agency and the work it is doing? If some unfortunate incident occurs—a suicide, a teenage pregnancy, a rash of runaways, destruction of community property, or theft—what unfavorable publicity may result, and how will the community and the church view these events? How can an ever-increasing budget be justified to a lay board when the agency is not serving ever-increasing numbers of children? How can an influential parent who wants his youngster admitted be appeased when at a particular time there is no space for the youngster, or when the agency does not come close to being a suitable placement for that youngster?

The list of potential problems goes on and on, and fortunately they do not all converge at the same time. But they occur with enough regularity and intensity to render an agency vulnerable. An agency may become so preoccupied with defensive maneuvering to protect itself from real and fantasized attackers that defensiveness becomes the prevailing mode of operation.

This kind of frontline (office) mobilization may divert attention from much-needed program modification in many important areas, with the result that the quality of the program for the children deteriorates while public relations are being patched and a pseudoimage of excellence is projected. It sometimes even happens that the imagemakers become believers in the false or distorted image they have projected and then cannot afford to see the often poor quality of care the children actually receive. Such a system of tensions will not continue indefinitely, but it produces a most unhealthy environment while it does last; and recovery is an excruciatingly slow process.

The best and probably the only preventive approach is to keep the focus always on improving the quality of programs for the children. There are many tested principles of child care on which we can rely. These principles are those that promote growth and development in all spheres, and they must remain basic. At the same time an atmosphere is needed in which new and more refined approaches can be tried in a carefully planned manner.

If the quality of the program for the children can be maintained and improved, and if the agency holds this function paramount, "projecting an image" presents no great concern. The agency's image cannot be ignored, but it can be strengthened by a continual process of education for those who view the program from different angles of vision. The educational effort should be concerned with the agency's purpose, goals, and present capabilities accurately projected. This continuing quality of reality and candor can produce many allies for the agency in its efforts in behalf of children and may result in others aiding the agency to find ways and means for improving and expanding the solid work that is already going on for children and their parents. This stance will not eliminate criticism, but it does contribute to a more realistic appraisal of such criticism with the possibility of constructive use of it.

In seeking to improve the program, it is good to remember that there are always new theories, new techniques, shortcut schemes peddled by smooth hucksters, sweeping the country. Often, all that is new is the ballyhoo, but one sometimes sees a wholesale switch in children's programs to the latest "technique" being hawked in the marketplace of commonality.

We should look at these new approaches, but with a critical eye. Is it really new, or is it a derivative of existing theory, the only difference being that a part of a broader theory is highlighted in such dazzling light as to obscure its origins? There is undoubtedly something to be learned and used from therapy systems that have mass appeal and are promoted with missionary zeal. But the source of illumination may fade rapidly when the expected "salvation" does not take place. To sort out what is really new and mold it with the workable old appears to be a reasonable view.

What a children's home desperately needs in order to have any chance of carrying out its mission is an effective level of communication, particularly among its staff and also with the larger community. This implies a total awareness of what the program is about as well as the possession of skills and capabilities for reaching the goals of the institution. If these conditions exist, a prevailing therapeutic attitude is possible, and every facet of the program will contribute to the optimal growth and development of the children. Without these conditions, a program is likely to become a mere holding operation, a way station where plastic human freight is unloaded for a time before being hauled away.

To conclude, anyone charged with the creation of a therapeutic milieu, whether it be in a children's home, a residential treatment center, a group home, or some other variation, is up against a formidable task. There are so many parts to such an undertaking that assembling them into a workable system is complex indeed. Although these residential centers have many aspects in common, each is different from the other. There are many common principles of child care undergirding these treatment places, and many of their problems are common to all. Yet each center is unique in many ways, and this uniqueness reflects the context in which it is established.

Although the task is formidable, the successes can be enormously gratifying to all concerned. For success to occur, an entire staff must be invested in the program to the extent that it can take pride in the outcome, which should be the improved functioning of the children in the center's care. When this happens, each staff person will know that he or she had a small part in making it possible. The staff members will be secure enough within themselves and will have reached a sufficient level of maturity that the "I" of the individual is not threatened by the collective "we" of the staff.

CHAPTER 2

Meeting the Needs of Child-Care Workers

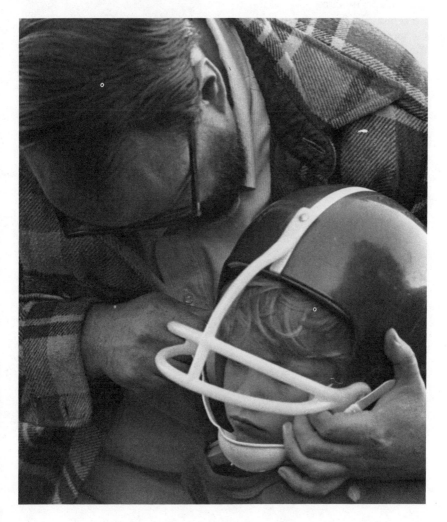

From whom the most is expected

WHEN WE LAY HELPLESS

Out of our long infancy
When we lay helpless
And would have perished
But for systems
Of personal support
We archaically cling
To remote images
Of someone caring
Traces of importance
Etched in neurons

Were it not for this
In an age of undoing
When we are caressed
But comforted not
By mechanical monsters
We should warp and die
Not by degrees
But all at once
Eliminating hypertrophied
Artifacts of personhood
Adaptational outcomes
Of marketplace reciprocity

While we secretly harbor
Ancient dreams
Unrecapturable
Yet unfaceable

One of the most difficult problems faced by children's homes is the finding, supporting, keeping, and upgrading of the child-care personnel. These people are identified by numerous titles: house-parents, counselors, child-care workers, mental health assistants, and so on. Patterns of staffing differ greatly, from the eight-hour shift to "living in" around the clock for extended periods of time.

What all these people have in common is that they are "on the firing line" with the children for far greater blocks of time than any other staff members. They are absolutely vital if any program of child care is to succeed beyond the mere basics of providing food and a place to sleep for very troubled youngsters. Providing these benefits is a great contribution to the welfare of some of these youngsters, but it is not enough for most of them. The efforts of child-care workers can promote health or hinder it.

What is alarming is that in many children's homes this category of personnel is the one from which the most is expected but which receives the least attention, is the first to be blamed when some-thing goes wrong, and is the most poorly understood and nurtured.

In many instances it is surprising that these people manage to be as effective as they are. It is the child-care worker, when he or she has been effective with a given child while in residence, who later receives a letter, a telephone call, a word-of-mouth greeting, or an unexpected visit from the youngster. Two lives have been touched in some unforgettable way.

No two institutions approach the problems of the child-caring personnel in exactly the same manner, because each institution is different. And there may be no ideal solution to the problems because any child-care group is in a process of evolutionary change. It is a component of a larger network and is influenced by surrounding change, both near and remote.

Let us consider the changes that have occurred over a four-year period in one children's center. Some of the functions will be described because it appears that these changes have resulted in a higher level of individual and group satisfaction and, consequently, in improved care for troubled youngsters.

This institution is a center for disturbed children of preadoles-cent age, though it is possible for a particular child to remain in residence into the early teen years, depending on size, nature of disturbance, level of maturity, and interests. This is the exception, however, as the program is not geared for the adolescent, and the youngster who moves into adolescence in a relatively mature manner is in danger of being isolated from needed peer interaction. If for sound reasons a child does remain beyond preadolescence, an effort is made to provide him or her with a more desirable supplementary milieu through attendance at a public school and participation in community group activities such as Scouts and church groups, which provide a more nearly normal setting for peer interaction.

This institution was formerly an orphanage of long standing, but more recently it has maintained a steady effort to become a treatment center in its own right. As with many similar places undergoing change, it has had its share of organizational crises, in some measure thought to be related to an uncertain philosophical base. For example, there was widespread and continuing disagreement among frequently changing key staff members as to the length of time a child should remain in residence, the tendency being to keep extending the time in residence.

At the same time, the staff displayed varying conceptions of what should constitute an active treatment plan for the children. Clinical staff placed a high value on cognitively outlining a treatment plan for each child, but often this was largely a front-office exercise with minimal attention paid to continuous execution of the plan. Reports indicate that key staff was prone to shift quickly from one school of thought to another in its search for an optimal approach to treatment, veering from a pseudopsychoanalytical approach to operant conditioning, reality therapy, transactional analysis, gestalt therapy, and so on ad infinitum.

Meanwhile, one suspects that the words rolled on and the focus was more search centered than child centered. Perhaps this is all a part of the quest for an identity that every institution of similar nature must seek. What, in fact, appears to happen is that the "transition" becomes a steady state and no condition of therapeutic effectiveness is ever found. If this condition persists, without stabilizing and melding workable approaches from many schools of thought, a staff instability develops that can be, in many ways, destructive to the child in residence. No magic is involved in developing a therapeutic program, but it is a prime necessity that the institution be capable of both assimilation and accommodation of input from both within and without the organization. Underlying all this must be always the paramount questions of what the multiple causative factors contributing to the child's malfunctioning are and what the staff can do to help reduce the grip of these noxious factors. At the same time, one must ask what the strengths of the child are and how the staff can facilitate their growth and consolidation and thereby increase the child's coping abilities. If one only keeps these questions uppermost, the program becomes child centered rather than method oriented, and the "school of thought" controversy among therapies requires much less emotional ego investment by staff, with the result that there are far fewer continuing intramural battles and consequent emotional casualties at all levels. Fewer staff members leave in anger, hurt, or despair; less energy is spent in tilting at windmills; and a coordinated effort is made to be of help to children in residence.

In other words, an environment is created that is conducive to the personal growth and development of the children rather than being an unreasonable replication of the unstable environment from which they have come. They need as models problem-solving adults rather than crusading actors in search of a self.

A dominant characteristic among the child-care workers at the center was the high level of frustration. When the writer was first directly acquainted with this institution, there had been a staff upheaval in the recent past, and several key professional staff members had left. They were replaced with new clinical staff, which was in the process of its own shakedown as to "who did what to whom with which," and once again the process of accommodating to one another and establishing territories and jurisdictions had resulted in frayed nerves. Some reasonable state of compromise had to be reached before the staff could be expected to begin to deal effectively with the problems of the child-care workers.

The frustration of child-care staff was obvious even to a casual observer and expressed itself in many ways. For instance, at meetings of all kinds many child-care workers demanded to be told what to do about a particular child. There was high resistance to trying to review a situation and look for clues that might reveal what had contributed to a particular crisis. Moreover, daily power struggles developed between counselors and children, which resulted in frequent and prolonged use of the isolation room. It was not unusual for one to pass this room, far removed from the activities areas, and find a child alone and sobbing, or cursing and beating the walls. To make matters worse, the child would usually be unattended; if not, there was no sight line through which to see the person outside the room. Alternatives were sometimes used, but too frequently the crisis built until the child was completely devastated and out of control and the child-care person was almost in the same condition. Moreover, the alternative of corporal punishment was generously administered.

In addition, staff expectations were high, and the pressure exerted for performance was often more than a child could bear. It was almost as though the staff disregarded completely the fact that the child had many problems. Whether intended or not, attitudes often conveyed the idea of "He's a bad child and is doing this deliberately." Behavior not desired by staff was called manipulation. No doubt there was manipulative behavior by some children, but one often wondered who manipulated most, children or staff.

Physical complaints of children were frequently shrugged off with attitudinal statements such as "He just wants attention; there's nothing wrong with him." Even if this assessment were correct, the child often was rejected and the attention mentioned was not provided.

A frequent complaint of child-care workers at this time was that they were isolated from the rest of the staff. Too frequently, when they needed someone to turn to for help in a particular situation, no one was available. They felt unimportant in the program as far as the front office was concerned. Child-care staff turnover rate was quite high, and a new worker was often put to work with no real program of orientation. Often, the new worker's high anxiety level spread to the children in the cottage, and it was easy for inexperienced workers to become overwhelmed with frustration in the relative isolation.

Assistant child-care workers were on a "rotating" or "floating" basis. That is, they were assigned regularly to no specific cottage but filled in wherever needed when a senior child-care worker was ill or off duty. This practice resulted in sporadic assignment to a group of children with whom the worker might have no acquaintance at all, and certainly no continuity of relationship. It should be added that the programmed day at the center was such that clinical staff members (social workers, psychologist, nurse, child-care supervisor, and director) were on duty during regular daytime hours from about 8:00 A.M. to 5:00 P.M. five days a week. Child-care workers on the other hand, began their work late in the afternoon, with the exception of about an hour at noon when they were present in the cottage to serve meals prepared in the central kitchen. Thus, there was very little opportunity for exchange with the rest of the staff, and a child-care worker frequently would begin work with minimal or no information as to what kind of day the children had been through. They also had little information about children's visits away from the center and, in fact, little coordinated information about the children.

Above and beyond these specifics, there are always latent concerns in almost any group of child-care workers. Some have been unable to find other jobs and soon become disgruntled at finding themselves in a low-paying, long-hours work situation that is quite limited in terms of economic or status advancement within the organization. Others, who are there out of some need to care for and help children, find the pace of recovery by these children too slow and soon begin to feel that they are contributing nothing or that other staff members are inhibiting their therapeutic work. In either instance, the workers are prone to develop feelings and attitudes, out of their own needs, that are not health promoting for the children. Still others who become involved in this kind of work are consciously or unconsciously looking for therapeutic help for themselves and view the "cloistered institution" as a haven from the world or as a place where professional staff will supply the ill-defined help for which they are searching. Sometimes such a bid for therapy is flattering to an inexperienced director or to a young professional worker, and the ensuing relationships can have far-reaching dissonant effects on the network of persons trying to create a therapeutic milieu for children. Generally it is possible to direct a staff member to a suitable outside agency or person if such help is needed. One hopes that the overall experience of being a child-care worker is growth promoting, but this is quite different from trying to use the job to treat one's own problems.

Gradually, in this situation, an observer could become aware of changes in behavior and activities that reflected a change in orientation and attitude among these workers. These changes were often subtle in quality and sometimes appeared briefly and then disappeared. It is not the single incident but the clustering of such incidents and the spread among the group that is significant. Of importance too is that such incidents are sustained by the group.

Some concrete examples of incidents observed at this center during the year will give an idea of how things have progressed. There has been, for instance, a marked shift in the quality of staff discussion of a particular problem about a particular child. The prevailing kind of inquiry now goes something like this: "Tommy is causing me a problem. Will you help me to understand him better so that we can figure out how to help him?" The question is put calmly, and the child-care worker appears to have the child's need in focus. This is not to say that workers' feelings are never ruffled—far from it—but inquiries are rational and concerned with trying to be of help to the children. The exaggerated anger and the attitude of being "put upon," the "it's the child or me" power-struggle situation, have been greatly diminished. The suppression of behavior by threat or rejection has been lessened.

At the same time there has been a greatly decreased use of the isolation room.[1] Use of this room is a rare occurrence now, and even when it is used the attitudes and practices are different. The child is not left as if in banishment for his unacceptable behavior but may rejoin activities when he appears to be in control of his emotions. There is a sight line so that the child-care person can be seen by the child inside. If a child is put into the room the person who put him there usually stays outside the door and lets him know it. Or, if tolerated by the child, the adult may stay in the room while emotions settle down and talk over with the child the events surrounding the episode. There has been a corresponding decrease in corporal punishment.

1. The writer does not intend to condemn the idea of a time-out or isolation room. It can be used very positively for a child who has lost control, and it provides an opportunity for the discharge of feelings without disrupting others or without suffering the social downfall that may result when the child loses all control and is destructive and hurtful to other children, staff, and property. But in the situation we are discussing, the isolation room had been all too frequently used for punitive action.

Greater community involvement by counselors has shown itself in a number of ways. One such instance had to do with children's visits in the community. Many children at this center either have no visiting families or their own families live at such a great distance that frequent visits in either direction are impractical. Though the program of arranging visits with families in the community is in no way a function of the child-care workers, it was encouraging to see various child-care workers identify a child who needed this supplemental family and often assist informally in recruiting families through associations at church, a local university, or membership in other groups outside the center.

A second instance of community involvement focused around the program for perceptual-motor skills. A recreation specialist at the center has developed a most successful program for those children with perceptual-motor deficits. With the assistance of several child-care workers, he put together a live demonstration called the "Gross Motor Circus," which was presented at the State Council for Learning Disabilities meeting at a large hotel, and again at a large meeting of the President's Council for Physical Fitness at a local university. By arrangement the circus was videotaped by the university and has since been used as a teaching film. These presentations resulted in much favorable comment, and all concerned—children, recreator, and child-care staff—were much encouraged by the recognition given their work.

Another piece of creative work by two child-care workers has found an audience beyond the walls of the center. This is a thirty-minute film called "A World within a World," in which these workers have attempted through sight and sound to convey the impression of a child growing through the experiences at the center. This artistic production emphasizes that a children's program cannot be a closed system. It highlights the continual exchanges between the child and the larger community.

Some of these examples are concerned directly with day-to-day child care. Others move away from the microcosm of counselor-child and suggest an expanding awareness of the many elements in a successful child-care program. Implicit in all these examples, and others, is evidence that these particular child-caring persons have moved away from an egocentric position to the point where they are able to see more clearly the needs of a child and to conceptualize additional means of meeting these needs. Of major importance, too, is the implication that in some gratifying manner the needs of the child-caring group have been met more successfully. How does this take place, and more specifically, how has it happened in this instance?

It is almost axiomatic that group needs must be met to a reasonable degree before such a group can begin to meet the needs of socially and emotionally disturbed children. Of primary importance in meeting these group needs was the appointment of a child-care supervisor. Such a person is central to the satisfaction level achieved by child-care staff. The supervisor becomes the advocate for the child-care staff and is largely responsible for integrating their efforts with total staff efforts. He is the one who must listen to the child-care workers and permit them to have impact on the program. He is the person who must experience their frustrations and share in their pleasures. The center was fortunate to find a man with considerable experience in working with children with social and emotional problems.

Initially, the supervisor of child care scheduled a weekly hour of individual supervision with each child-care worker. This was designed to help clarify in a continuing manner the role of child-care worker for a new employee. It was a time for feedback in both directions, which was most beneficial. For the child-care workers it was reassuring to know that some part of their work was considered effective, and discussion of specific interpersonal problems increased the inner armamentaria of the workers and widened their fields of awareness. The supervisor in turn received many suggestions about modification of program, which he was in a position to explore with other staff and to provide feedback and often to effect change in some facet of the program.

As other teaching functions solidified and counselors gained experience, supervision became much more informal, often occurring on an as needed basis at the instigation by either child-care workers or supervisor. As a matter of fact, there is a high level of peer supervision at this time.

With the financial remuneration for child-care workers relatively low, it is unrealistic to expect that such a population will remain fixed for any great length of time. They come and they go; but a few, for reasons peculiar to individual circumstances, will remain in these positions for an extended time. The younger individuals rarely remain beyond a year or two.

Because every person comes to such a position with widely differing experiences, and because few have had any formal training in child care, it becomes doubly important for a child-care agency to make every effort to develop a continuing in-service program that will contribute to the formation of a health-promoting milieu that remains after individual workers are gone. This provides a pattern of attitudes and actions from which new child-care workers can borrow and on which they can model their own performance. At the same time it sets up expectations and a cultural pool of knowledge and wisdom, thus removing some of the anxiety that arises when a new person comes to work and tries to find his way both toward effectiveness as a child-care worker and toward a comfortable level of satisfaction in such work.

In-service training at this center has taken several forms, all of them significant and together forming a network of continual training. These have included:

1. *Seminars conducted by the child-care supervisor for a two-hour period once each week.* Content of these seminars has been wide-ranging—child growth and development, children's feelings, ways of responding to children's questions, staff feelings, importance of family to children, and so on.
   At first they were conducted entirely by the supervisor with group discussion and inquiry. As the group became more familiar with this ongoing learning process, staff members from all areas of the program were invited to lead seminars. In this way child-care staff become more aware of other facets of the total program and problems peculiar to other areas, such as recreation, school, psychotherapy, and nutrition. The staff also was able to see more clearly how a dysfunction in one area could signal trouble ahead in another area.
   A milestone was reached when the child-care group presented a seminar for all other staff on "What It Is Like to Be a Child-Care Worker." The seminar was a combined effort of the child-care staff, with one person condensing and presenting the many views. This event had much to do with

moving the total staff closer together in its function of helping disturbed children.

This was the beginning of further cooperation. The child-care staff is now often responsible for its own training seminar, with one or two persons preparing material for the group. Staff members from other areas are welcome to attend if they wish, and they often do. Likewise, counselor staff is welcome to attend other group presentations.

2. *Treatment-planning conferences, which take place within a week or two after a child has come into residence.* Representatives from all staff areas, especially child-care staff, contribute to these conferences by identifying the child's strengths and problem areas. At this time a tentative treatment plan is formulated for an individual child.

3. *Treatment conferences held regularly for each child every three months.* These conferences are designed to review progress, to provide a total staff involvement in updating treatment plans or in formulating guidelines for discharge to home or alternative placement, and to suggest special attention (school, clinic, and so on) the child may need after leaving the center. These conferences serve a valuable teaching function for the entire staff and provide a system of checks and balances on staff perceptions and attitudes, and the carrying out of treatment plans.

4. *Mini-staff conferences, held each morning.* Total staff available at that time review briefly some of the children who may be having particular problems.

5. *Impromptu conferences.* These are designed so that any staff member may have time with the consulting child psychiatrist to discuss concerns about a particular child. Child-care staff, teachers, and recreation workers, for example, often request such time. Sometimes a solution to the particular problem can be found, sometimes not. If a specific child is having trouble in many areas, several staff members may come together the following week for more comprehensive discussion

and planning for a particular child. Sometimes no change of plan appears necessary, ánd reassurance for the child-care worker is sufficient. Again, many positive and negative transferences develop between a child and the child-care worker, and sometimes the discussion may focus on these relationships and the ways in which the worker can help the child (and self) with these feelings. Often the attempt to put into perspective a child's own viewpoint, which depends on his unique life experiences, may be enough to aid the child-care worker in moving ahead with the child in a more therapeutic approach.

A change in staff assignment in the cottages also appears to have paid dividends. At one time the cottages were covered by individuals called "child-care workers" and "relief workers." Under this plan each cottage had coverage for five days out of eight by the regular counselor assigned to the cottage. On the three other days of an eight-day cycle, each cottage would have one relief worker for two days and still another for one day. This created problems for children, child-care workers, and programming. Children and relief workers did not know each other well, and inconsistency of attitude and management resulted.

Two co-child-care workers are now assigned permanently to each cottage, and this change has resulted in considerable reduction of conflict. These two persons are committed to their cottage and arrange between themselves for time off and vacations. This plan has resulted in smoother articulation with other facets of the total program. It has also made possible attendance and participation by at least one child-care worker at conferences of his or her choice during certain hours when child-care workers are not on duty, thereby contributing to a more harmonious working relationship with other staff.

Historically, child-care workers work long hours, but the current plan has many positive aspects. For example, after the changeover in the early morning to the day program (school, therapy, recreation, and so on), child-care workers are off duty until the noon hour when one of them returns to the cottage to serve lunch (prepared in the central kitchen). At one o'clock this person is free until late afternoon when the day program is finished. Then both return to duty, providing double coverage until after the children have gone to bed. During the children's peak hours of need—morning and early evening—two adults are present. One of the child-care workers "sleeps in" during the night, and the other returns to nearby quarters.

The idea of separate quarters for child-care staff is important, inasmuch as it provides the worker with his own territory during off-duty time. This eliminates a frequent complaint among child-care workers whose permanent quarters are in the children's cottages that even when they are off duty they have no privacy and no place for rejuvenation, a necessary consideration that often does not receive enough attention from administrators.

A most interesting observation has frequently been made about movement of children from one cottage to another since the current assignment plan went into operation. Traditionally, the decision about which cottage a child will live in has been a continuing problem. Plans to move a child from one cottage to another were often based on the frustration tolerance of a particular child-care worker, and such moves were met with resistance by other counselors who appeared to feel that they were being used by another cottage whose workers could not manage a difficult child.

This syndrome has almost disappeared under the current assignment plan. Fewer children are moved, and when a move does occur it is generally a cooperative, planned effort between cottages, with the needs of the child the foremost consideration. The child-care workers concerned work out what to them is a constructive and mutually acceptable plan before the matter is brought to the administrative office for action and before the child is told that he may move. Many moves are initiated by the children themselves, often for good reasons. Thus, the autonomy of the children is encouraged, and the child can take part in the rational decision making.

This system provides a high degree of flexibility in scheduling work time for child-care staff, encourages investment in the cottage, and sets a high level of expectation for the staff's ingenuity and cooperation, at the same time providing a framework for the autonomy necessary to execute such a plan. In addition to an improved emotional climate for the children, there are other positive benefits such as coordinated planning for trips and outings and weekend recreation. The level of cottage orderliness has vastly improved, and the amount of property destruction has diminished.

A major problem among children's homes that are evolving into treatment centers has been the noticeable lag in personnel practices. Persons who worked in children's homes in the bygone days of an agrarian way of life often made a lifelong career of this work. There may not have been great financial reward, but many perquisites (often unstated) went with the job. This is rarely true any longer, but even today there is some expectation that one does such work out of Christian dedication. It does nothing to depreciate the importance of dedication to suggest that this is a concept that may need analysis and updating. In a society that is achievement oriented on an economic basis, it appears that some increasing remuneration would reinforce an already existing dedication. This particular center, where all child-care staff received the same pay regardless of length of service, has now begun a gradual increment in pay for seniority and demonstrated effectiveness on the job. This may not be as great as desirable, but the improvement is real.

Further, the process of employing a child-care worker has changed. At one time employment was largely a front-office decision. Now at least three child-care workers interview a prospective colleague, and this function is rotated among all child-care workers. If, after discussing and evaluating all views with the assistant director, the child-care workers are opposed to hiring an applicant, he or she is not hired. This practice has resulted in much easier entry into the program for a new child-care worker. Several new workers have noted that when they first came to work other child-care workers were their most important teachers. They started work as allies of the present staff rather than as intruders imposed on the group from without.

Another helpful move has been promotion "from within" of a child-care worker to the position of assistant supervisor of child care. This speaks positively for the effective functioning of the child-care group as well as for the particular individual's efforts to increase his knowledge and skills, including pursuit of a graduate degree in his spare time. Although the center has had so many budgetary problems that support for further formal education has not been possible, administration has expressed the wish that this could be possible in the future.

Undergraduate and graduate programs are available locally to enable child-care workers to take courses that would better equip them for the work and that could lead to an undergraduate or graduate degree. Tuition support for such a work-related curriculum, or time off from work, appears to be a good agency investment. Many child-care workers probably would take advantage of such offerings, even if it meant that a contractual agreement would have to be made for an extended work commitment to the agency. Should one leave employment before that time was completed, there could be the option of repaying actual tuition costs. Meanwhile, the center has supported and encouraged attendance and participation by counselors in extramural workshops in child-related matters. This is one more instance of providing portals of communication between the institutional group and others engaged in similar work with children.

Partly as a result of this, and as the quality of the total program has improved and has been recognized by educational institutions in the area, requests for practicum experience for students have increased greatly. At any one time student counselor interns (graduate), student teachers (graduate and undergraduate), sociology and psychology students engaged in field work, and pediatric resident physicians may be found at the center. Although no formal teaching responsibility falls on the child-care worker, the child-care staff is in continual interaction with these students, affording it an additional involvement in an instructional capacity. This recognition that the child-care worker has information and experience worth imparting to others with less experience enhances the worker's view of self.

But perhaps the professional nature of the child-care workers' job is most clearly signaled by their use as cotherapists with their cottage groups. Each week all the children in a cottage have group therapy sessions. A recent change has included the child-care worker as coleader with a member of the clinical staff. These sessions are designed to explore children's feelings about events and interactions in their daily lives. Many different techniques are used, such as game simulation and psychodrama with role changes. Thus, the children gradually learn more about their own behavior and the impact of their behavior on others. Frequently, the feedback from others encourages them to make cognitive plans for changing their own behavior. Serving as cotherapist not only enhances the child-care worker's self-esteem but facilitates his or her own understanding of children and self. It is a valuable teaching-learning situation for all involved. As a child increases in ego strength, he may take a role as coleader of the group from time to time.

This has been an attempt to analyze the process by which the needs of child-care staff in one institution have been met rather successfully, thereby raising the level of effective performance. In the process we have noted the development of a group, with loyalties, goals, roles, and means of making decisions.

Such a process has occurred within the framework of an institution where the child-care staff receives both formal and informal feedback regarding its work; and, as the group has progressed, it has taken on more of the decisions that formerly were made outside the group. This democratic process has resulted in group cohesiveness and has imparted status not experienced before. The group has developed a life of its own. It is no longer a collection of individuals, each with his own agenda. A part of each has contributed something that has made the group more than the sum of its parts. It has also become much better articulated both with other components of the organization and with the larger community outside the institution.

There can be no doubt that the changes that have transpired in this group have led to a far higher level of morale than existed a few years ago, and there is now a kind of cultural blueprint (beliefs, values, patterns of behavior) that can be passed on in an orderly manner to subsequent child-care workers. These too will modify and change the blueprint, for change is continual, depending on the actors and the environment. The level of effective child care has greatly increased at the center, as would be obvious to even the casual observer.

A final comment might be that the functions of such a group can be greatly helped or hindered by the attitudes of the administrative staff. In this instance they have helped. We have seen how this group was aided by administration in acquiring tools through which it could change by a process of assimilation and accommodation. Yet, when such a group looks back, it can paraphrase the ancient Chinese philosopher Lao-tzu and say, "Why, we did that ourselves."

CHAPTER 3

Dog Gone

He remembered his one best friend

ONE BEST FRIEND

He remembered his one best friend
Named Ged when he was about five
Ged was the caretaker
At the junkyard across the tracks
Lived in a tarpaper shack
Worked at these odd jobs
Ged was retarded later he learned
Didn't know then didn't matter
Ged was his friend
But how did he know
He talked to me and listened
Let me pat his dog named Big
Never ran me away
Like all the others did

The Experience of a Cottage

The situation was touch and go for a group of early to midadolescent boys. During the previous two years they had come at
different times from widely separated areas to live in a children's
home. They lived in several cottages on the campus that operated
under the philosophy that each could at least simulate a family;
therefore, in each cottage there were early-latency boys and girls,
late-latency children, early- to midadolescents, and a scattering of
late adolescents. Conflict was the order of the day, and of the
night too, in each of these cottages. The majority of the so-called
houseparents left in despair, anger, or disgust. Many of them left
feeling that they had failed, and others left with the distinct impression that the institution had failed.

The institution, once an orphanage, had moved ten years before to a new campus on the periphery of the city. Very few of the
residents were actually orphans, and the institution was now called
a children's home. Social forces and changing times have brought
many modifications in children's institutions in recent years, and
this children's home had undergone rather rapid change. In fact,
there was talk from time to time that the program was going to
change in the near future from a children's home to a children's
treatment center. Most of the professional staff was new and the
rapid turnover of child-caring personnel and the sporadic mention
of change to a "treatment center" led to a high degree of anxiety.

Power struggles between houseparents and adolescent boys especially were rampant throughout the program. After many
discussions, it was decided that, as no specific program could be
identified for the adolescent boys, they would be moved from their
respective cottages to a single cottage, where it was hoped they
would be easier to manage.

But who would manage this group of boys? There was a young
man present whose wife had been the chief houseparent in the
cottage to which these boys were to be moved. The young man
had been attending graduate school at a nearby university, and the
couple lived in an apartment in the cottage. His graduate work
was nearly completed, and because his wife wanted to pursue further academic work this was a convenient time to make a change.
Prior to this, the administration had observed that when this

young man was present in the cottage he appeared to relate well with the children, and it was thought that he could be instrumental in creating a more desirable environment for these adolescent boys. Thus, Jones Cottage was designated for this group of adolescent boys. The husband and wife exchanged cottage roles: she went back to school, and he became the houseparent.

The adolescent boys shared backgrounds of deprivation, emotional and otherwise, and they were all spoken of as "acting-out youngsters." The usual panoply of descriptive terms would apply to the group as a whole: impulsiveness, difficulty in forming peer relationships, difficulty in relating to authority, hostile-aggressive attitudes, and lack of trust. When the plan to place them all together was made known to the boys, some of them were reluctant. Only one or two moved in at a time. However, over a period of two or three months, this cottage gained status in the eyes of the various boys around the campus, and pretty soon the eight beds were filled.

Each of the boys came from a broken home, and each had moved many times during his life. Max had lived with his mother for a few years in a chaotic household where the mother was absent for long periods of time, leaving him to fend for himself. When his father remarried in another city, he wanted to go to the wedding, but his mother told him that if he went he could not return to live with her. He attended the wedding and then began to live with his father, whom he had seen very little in recent years, and the stepmother, who had an eight-year-old daughter of her own. The new living situation was fairly calm at first but very quickly became one of continual conflict. Max felt left out, and there was much sibling rivalry. He began to act out in the community, to steal, and to fight frequently with peers. At times he was sad and depressed and at other times frantic.

Dawson had been adopted when he was about three years of age and had lived a relatively stable life until his adoptive father died. He believed, however, that his adoptive mother had never accepted him, and after the father's death he and the mother were in continual conflict. Many times he ran away from home. Occasionally, when he came home late at night, his mother locked him out and he spent the night on the porch. He had also become involved in drug usage (marijuana and occasional LSD). Prior to admission to the children's home, he had been in two foster homes, but each placement had failed rather quickly. He came to the children's home directly from the second foster home, where his repeated sniffing of gasoline had precipitated the move.

Dick had never known a home, as his family had disintegrated when he was a baby. He had lived in twelve foster homes during his first dozen years and had no continuing attachments. Although he had two brothers in a distant children's home he saw them very infrequently. There appeared to be poor sibling attachment among these children. When Dick was good he was very, very good, and when he was bad he was very bad. He was continually engaged in conflict and had an explosive temper. He bullied the younger children by hitting and intimidating them. He was a large, strong boy for his age, and most of the children on campus were afraid of his volatile temper and physical abusiveness. At times of explosion he was destructive toward property or person.

Bascom had been in several foster homes. Although he saw his mother and grandmother occasionally, he had no hope that he could live with either of them. His grandmother was aged and chronically ill; his mother had a severe alcohol problem and expressed no overt interest in this boy, despite many efforts by social workers over the years. Bascom had severe learning disabilities and had been totally frustrated in public schools.

Everett's mother had abandoned her family when he was a few years of age, and he had been reared during his early years by a paternal grandmother. His father had been in prison for larceny most of the boy's life. Everett, like Bascom, had many learning disabilities, and school was a source of great frustration for him. He was angry most of the time and was in continual conflict with any houseparents.

Ross was a small early adolescent, but he made up in cunning what he lacked in size. He had lived at home all of his life, though the family was problem laden. A short while before he came to the children's home, his family was in the process of disintegrating, and his parents separated soon after his admission. The initial referral was made on the advice of school personnel, where Ross was making no academic progress even though he was considered to be above average in intelligence. He ran away from school numerous times and was found, on more than one occasion, unconscious from wine obtained at a nearby shop.

Karl's father and mother separated when Karl was a baby. He did not remember seeing his father and had been told on a number of occasions that his father left home because Karl "was a boy," all the other children being girls. He did not want to believe this, but it bothered him. His mother soon remarried, and although the family was still together it was a very troubled one where overt conflict reigned. When Karl was a small boy, an aunt took him to live with her, and this was his principal base of operation, although at various times he went back to his family briefly until mounting tension prompted him to run away to his aunt's.

Lance was the last to move into the cottage, and he, like Ross, was small in stature; despite this, he was also something of a leader. His family had broken up when he was quite small, and a maternal aunt had maintained an intermittent interest in the boy. He saw his father, who lived alone, from time to time and could get along with him all right when the father was not drinking; but as Lance said, "My father drinks most of the time, and I couldn't live there." He did not know the whereabouts of his mother.

So it was a motley assortment of young adolescents who eventually moved into Jones Cottage. Within a few months their discordant presence around campus began to diminish, and there was evidence on all sides that some group loyalty was forming. Although conflict was always there, it was obvious that the boys had begun to function somewhat as a group and to negotiate some matters of conflict verbally rather than allowing each disagreement to result in fisticuffs or destruction of property. To a boy, they all appeared to think highly of their housefather and to hold him in esteem and respect. In response to a question about the qualities that made Rod a good housefather, Lance said: "He likes us, and that makes us like him. When we do something wrong, he will talk with us and treat us like people. He never screams and yells at us. The others always scream and yell, and most of us have been screamed and yelled at all of our lives." The others echoed Lance's view.

Rod continued as housefather for nearly a year, but his personal plans were unsettled. He debated whether to pursue further academic work or to seek another job with more possibility of advancement. Either course would involve a move. After several weeks of uncertainty, Rod decided in mid-February to resign, and a date for his leaving was arranged for the end of the month.

It was hard for Rod to leave, and he had difficulty telling the boys about it, though some of them already suspected it. The presence, by this time, of a reliable assistant, Sherman, made the parting a little easier for the housefather and the boys. Rod was on the scene a couple of times shortly after the move when he returned with his van to take his and his wife's belongings to another state.

The boys had formed some attachment to Sherman, and it was the general consensus among observers that Rod and Sherman had worked very well together as housefathers. The boys were concerned about whether or not Sherman would stay after Rod left. One of the boys said, "I'm just afraid that Sherman will get fed up and we'll find a note tacked to the door some morning, telling us that he has had it and that he can't take it anymore; then we'll be all alone." This did not happen, but their grief over Rod's leaving was prolonged.

The boys said that Rod had promised that when he and his wife were settled in another state and he had a job they would definitely make plans for the boys to come at various times to visit them. They, in turn, would come back to the children's home to visit. This seemed to ease the pangs of separation somewhat for the boys and was a constant subject of conversation among them for weeks. Also, one frequently heard the comment, "Rod's coming back, you know. He left his dog Kristie. He loved Kristie, and you know he'll come back to get Kristie one of these days. I sure would like to see Rod."

Kristie was a duke's mixture of a dog, and no one knew her origins exactly. When she first arrived, she would charge across the field toward the boys, suddenly coming to a stop twenty or thirty feet away, where she would stand, looking frightened. It was as though she wanted to be friendly with the boys but was afraid. This gradually changed, and she became a willing and eager participant in the boys' activities. One of the boys said, "You know, I like Kristie. She's not like a lot of dogs. I don't like purebred dogs. What I like is a mutt, and Kristie is a mutt."

Another boy said, "Kristie is just like a person. When you're happy, Kristie is happy with you. When you're sad, Kristie is sad, too. Many is the time when I've been worried or troubled about something, I'd take Kristie for a walk and sit down under a tree and talk to her just like I talk to you. She seemed to understand, and it helps me a lot just to be with Kristie and to talk to her."

One late spring afternoon a pickup truck with enclosed canopy turned off the boulevard to the children's home and stopped briefly in front of the administration building where the driver inquired of a younger child as to the location of Jones Cottage. He drove around to the front of the cottage and asked one of the boys who was outside where the dog was they wanted him to pick up.

"What are you talking about?" the boy asked brusquely.

"I don't know what dog it is, but someone called for me to come pick up a dog that you wanted to get rid of."

"We don't want to get rid of no dog," the boy said loudly. By that time, other residents of the cottage were coming out to see what the noise was about.

"We ain't got no dog," another boy said firmly.

"There must be a dog here somewhere that you want me to pick up or they wouldn't have called about it."

"Nobody here owns a dog, mister. There's only one dog around here, and it belongs to Rod—and you can't have Rod's dog. He's coming back to get his dog."

By that time Sherman had shown up, and he told the driver that it was true there was a dog and that he had called the dogcatcher. At about that time, Kristie ran from behind the cottage and stopped several feet from the group. The dogcatcher started over to the dog, and instantly two or three of the boys ran in front of him and started pushing him back. The other boys ran into the field, calling Kristie to come with them. The dogcatcher made another attempt, and one of the smaller boys grabbed him and started cursing him. Sherman tried to reason with them, and soon everyone was involved in a shouting, name-calling scene. The dogcatcher told Sherman he would come back another day, as the boys were so uncooperative.

Later, one of the boys said they had waited until dark and then had taken Kristie to a treehouse they had built a couple of hundreds yards from the cottage. Kristie stayed there overnight. They fed her the next morning, and the plan was that a couple of them would skip school that day and stay in the woods with Kristie to keep the dogcatcher from taking her. The housefather, however, prevailed, and they all went to school reluctantly. The dogcatcher came sometime during that day, and when the boys returned from school and found the dog gone the pandemonium began all over again. They couldn't understand why someone was giving Rod's dog away when Rod had clearly said that he was going to come back and get his dog.

Jones Cottage was not the most well-kept cottage on campus from the point of view of orderliness and cleanliness, and this event took place a couple of days before the state inspectors were due to arrive for a site visit related to accrediting part of the institution as a treatment center for emotionally and socially disturbed children. The administration had directed the housefather to have the cottage thoroughly cleaned. Also, he was instructed to get rid of the dog, which spent a good part of its time in the cottage, especially when the boys were there.

Anger over the dog's removal continued. A couple of the boys would not even speak to the housefather, and one boy later reported that he did not speak to Sherman for over a month after the incident. Others who were more vocal called him every name they could think of. Even though he explained over and again the situation they were up against, he was the focal point, along with the dogcatcher, of their wrath. They also included the director of the home in their verbal attacks, but none of them talked with him directly.

The housefather was disturbed about having to get rid of Kristie, and he immediately talked with administration about the loss of the dog, which obviously meant much to the boys. The boys evolved a plan whereby they would pool their allowances and bring Kristie back from the dog pound. They called the person in charge of the pound, who agreed that he would hold Kristie for them.

By the time the inspection was over, the boys had pooled their quarters and had the necessary five dollars to pay for reclaiming Kristie. Several of them accompanied the housefather in the home's van to the dog pound across town, and it was a joyous ride indeed. However, on arriving at the pound they were informed that someone had come looking for a dog and had promised to provide Kristie a good home. The boys' anger, temporarily abated, erupted anew, and they created quite a scene at the dog pound. They were angry with the people there, and they wanted to know where Kristie was. They would steal her back if necessary. They were offered a choice of other dogs at the pound, but this only made them angrier. They wanted Kristie, Rod's dog, and no other dog would do. Finally, the housefather was able to calm them enough to get them in the van to return to the children's home. It was an emotion-laden group of boys, some cursing, some sullen, and some crying.

The two months before the dogcatcher incident had been unsettled ones throughout the campus, especially in Jones Cottage. There had been talk by administration from time to time about converting the children's home to a children's treatment center. Nevertheless, there were many starts and stops, as is common in this kind of transition. It was common knowledge around campus, amplified by fantasy and rumor, that major changes would take place. The older children, adolescents, would be phased out of the program and only latency-age children would be admitted. No definite timetable was ever established for the transition; it would be more a gradual process than an abrupt change. Whether the reasons were founded in fact or not, it was the general impression that adolescents in the program would be "going somewhere" by the end of the school year or at least during the summer. Most of these adolescents had no place to go, and they were all unsettled about the prospect. Whenever they had a chance to talk to anyone, they expressed their feelings about the changes in the program that were being talked about by administration. One of the boys expressed the views of many in a statement that went somewhat as follows: "I have lived a lot of places and never belonged anywhere. Since I have been here, especially since I have been in Jones Cottage, I feel that I belong somewhere. I am getting along a lot better, but I am not ready to go out into the world and make it on my own at fifteen. I think it's wrong not to let us know just what is going to take place and when it is going to take place. If we have to leave we ought to know way ahead of time so we could get used to it and not have to worry about it all of the time. It scares the hell out of you to think about leaving the only place that you ever felt you belonged. I have no place to go, and I can't make it on my own at fifteen. It's just not right."

For several days after the loss of Kristie, the boys continued planning strategy for reacquiring her, but in the process of discussion they decided that Kristie probably had a good home and that it would be unfair to her to steal her away from the new owner. Besides, they were concerned about themselves. Where would they go when the changeover came from adolescents to younger children?

The unsettled conditions of the late winter and spring extended into early summer. Through the efforts of the housefather, Sherman, who was generally liked by these boys, another dog was acquired, a handsome golden retriever. They liked this dog, but the new dog never had the same meaning for them as Kristie had had.

During the weeks immediately following Kristie's removal by the dogcatcher, the boys' ambivalence toward their former houseparent, Rod, expressed itself in several ways—most clearly, perhaps, in Karl's comment: "Rod didn't care anything about Kristie in the first place, or he wouldn't have left her here so long. If he'd cared for Kristie, the dogcatcher wouldn't have had to be called. I guess he didn't care anything about us either, or he would have come back to visit like he said and to get Kristie. He told us we could come to visit him, but we haven't heard anything from him either. It's just been a bad time."

As time passed, the anger toward the dogcatcher and Sherman appeared to diminish. Nevertheless, an undercurrent of anxiety and anger continued about the impending changes in the program. This became the focus of their verbalizations, which were accompanied by frequent outbreaks of defiance of the authority of the institution. There were prolonged and unexcused absences from the campus during the day and night. At one time the boys brought friends from school and community for a direct confrontation with the home's administrative officers. It was an angry mob protesting the unfairness of forcing the adolescents to leave the home during the change to a treatment center. The police were called in to deal with the belligerent outside reinforcements. These behaviors led to dismissal of half the group from Jones Cottage, the older ones for the most part, and to implied threats to the others that they were in danger of having to leave also.

This story, apparently that of the loss of a dog, touches briefly on many other critical issues in group child care. One is the fallacy of trying to use "the family" as the model when cottages are woefully understaffed and houseparents are often untrained. Usually they must work interminably long hours to the point of exhaustion. Furthermore, the children are of varying ages from diverse backgrounds but with a commonality of deprivation. In such a setting it would be difficult to create a constructive "family." There is always the danger, especially when houseparents' tenure is brief, that the cottage living situation may become a real-life caricature of the family situations from which many of these children have come. Another critical issue is the failure in many child-caring institutions to provide a programmed day for moderate to extremely ego-damaged individuals who are quite incapable of providing their own healthful structure. These children, on an unconscious level, tend to perpetuate the chaos they have known for most of their lives.

It was salutary indeed that these boys were moved to Jones Cottage and that some of them had a period of time in which to observe Rod as a housefather from a distance, to invest themselves, and to have some part in deciding that they would like to belong to that group. There are indications that these boys were able to begin functioning as a group, with some loyalty and concern for each other, and at least to begin to develop a greater capacity for performing within the group and sustaining group efforts. The fact that Rod took this post by mutual agreement suggests the very important point of trying to effect a match between houseparents and particular children.

The importance of a child-caring institution in providing a period of stability for unstable youth cannot be overemphasized. The awareness of some of the boys of their tenuous affectional attachments in the past is clearly stated in some of their comments, and the comments about "belonging somewhere for the first time in my life" emphasize the value the boys placed on these relationships and attachments. From such a very basic beginning, good treatment and rehabilitation can proceed.

The rites of passage in a children's institution—that is, separation, transition, and incorporation—are in continual enactment. Each of these stages overlaps for any individual child, and some of the comments made by the boys suggest the extreme importance of staff attention to these different stages. The boys' overwhelming anxieties and fears about having to leave the institution are poignantly stated. The increasing frequency of the statement, "This place doesn't care anything about us," is stark evidence of the importance of detailed attention to separation. "What happened to Kristie is just what will happen to us. Someone will come with a net and take us somewhere that we don't want to go" was how one boy expressed his concerns.

The rapid turnover of "on-the-line" personnel, child-caring personnel, is a continuing problem in many institutions. Undoubtedly, it is related to many causative factors, but among the most common are lack of any continuing in-service training program and lack of day-to-day clinical and administrative support. With the rapid turnover of personnel, one wonders not that so many children make such poor adaptations but that some do quite well. The half-formed attachments occur with such frequency and regularity that the best many institutions can do is re-create the ghosts of the past. That some children show and are able to maintain improvement may, many times, speak more for the resilience of the human spirit than for the quality of child care at the institution.

Change is inevitable in a children's institution, whether planned or unplanned; and any kind of change always makes someone uncomfortable, and someone may be hurt in the process. Looking back on the sustained levels of anxiety, fear, and anger expressed among this group of boys about the idea of transition from the children's home (where adolescents had been able to remain for an indefinite period of time) to a treatment center for younger children, we can see that these anxieties and fears were very real to these boys. Not one of them had family to which he could return with any hope of reintegration. Though some of the families had been involved in casework, the involvement was far too slight and little had been accomplished. Many reality factors led to this situation, and certainly repeated attempts were made to work with any family where there was even a remote possibility of the boy's return.

At the same time, the adolescents were not taken into confidence, and little attention was paid to their anxieties by the higher-level administration. Child-caring personnel attempted to deal with the problem, as did some members of the clinical staff, but the fact is that these staff members did not have full information either. Staff anxiety was obvious, and the boys probably reacted to it. One boy said, "If anybody knows anything about the change, we think they should tell us; and they should listen to what we think about the situation. If we have to leave, we have to know ahead of time, and we have to have some kind of plan."

The children's despair and depression reached the point where apparently they had to take some action. One interpretation of their defiant behavior in recruiting support from some classmates in public school and community peers would be that some action, even though potentially destructive to them, was better than no action at all. It did result in some dismissals and threats to the younger adolescents who were likewise involved, but it was only after these dire events that long-needed attention was given to the voices of the adolescents remaining.

Several months after Rod and his wife had moved to another state, he did return for a visit. Though some of the boys were gone, those remaining were glad to see him and eager to tell him of the upheavals of the previous months. There was no overt indication that the remaining adolescents continued to feel rejected by Rod because he had not returned sooner, and they appeared to understand the reality of his life situation in a new job several hundred miles away. Although it may have made the situation more difficult in the beginning for Sherman, it undoubtedly was of some value in helping them in this transitional time to know that Sherman and Rod were good friends. Rod did write to Sherman from time to time, and Sherman shared this information with the boys during those months. This undoubtedly was of help to them also.

At the time of the dismissal of the older boys, there was genuine concern among all those remaining as to what would happen to the dismissed boys. One of the boys returned after nine months for a brief visit, and those present were all very pleased to see him and to know how matters had gone for him. The returning boy inquired about Rod and expressed many positive feelings about the time when Rod was the housefather. All the adolescents who were dismissed have somehow managed widely separated telephone calls to their former cottage.

Though it was a most difficult time, the remaining boys appear to have matured to some extent through the experience and have in fact been of considerable assistance to new and younger boys entering the program. The time is approaching when these boys will leave, and a great deal of attention is being given to preplanning and having the boys participate in the plans that will be available to them.

Although many of the highly charged feelings surrounding those months of upheaval have markedly subsided, they have not entirely disappeared. It was of interest that Lance, six months after the events under discussion, requested regular appointments with a psychiatrist. Almost a year to the day after Rod had gone, Lance wanted to talk about the time with Rod and the events following his departure. Lance said, "Rod liked us, and we liked him. He listened to us. When we did something wrong, he would talk to us and not treat us like dogs."

For this group of adolescent boys, wherever they are and whatever they will be, one suspects that always there will be a memory of that year with Rod. It provided them with a level of stability and care that had been missing from all of their lives.

Kristie was a symbol of remembered past losses and of the march of events in young lives over which there is frequently no control.

CHAPTER 4

Crisis Treatment of a Youth

He needed a place to sleep, to eat,
to learn the best he could

THE CONTRACT

I

His early years were spent
with a man and his wife
the father we shall call him
brought the baby boy
home from a hospital
never spoke of the boy's origins
the boy never questioned
and never knew

In a few years
the man's wife died
the boy remembers now
is saddened at the memory
the father we shall call him
soon married another woman
who brought many children
but soon she left
and the boy was glad

From then until fifteen
he took care of his father
brought him wine on request
from the corner grocer
worried that the man was dead
until he learned the difference
between passing out
and dying all at once

School was a nightmare
sometimes no clothes
sometimes truancy when teased
or chastised because he smelled
they moved from time to time
fleeing always at night
before the rent was due
when there was no money

The boy wrote in awkward hand
when asked his reasons
for wanting to come to stay
at the children's home

he stated simply
that he needed a place to sleep
needed food to eat
that he would like to learn
in exchange for all of this
he would work hard
give no trouble
and learn the best he could

II

Through fifteen and sixteen
after he came
he kept his words
every one of them
worked at odd jobs
was a friend to all
old and young alike
admired respected

He never left the grounds
except for school
and once in awhile
to visit his ailing father
about whom he never talked
fact is he went his daily way
talked of nothing in the past
of little in the future
and kept his contract

At seventeen the worker said
the boy was too dependent
on the children's home
so to toughen him up
prepare him for the future
he was sent against his will
to a swamp survival school
but he went quietly
in his quiet way

With his strong physique
he'd make it fine they said

but severe recurring headaches
brought him back in three days
on reaching the home
his headache went away
so he was dispatched at once
to find a summer apartment
that and a job it was said
would toughen him up
and weaken his need
to cling to the home

While searching without protest
that long afternoon
for a summer apartment

his sight blurred and
suddenly he was blind
the doctor and the staff
at the children's home
helped to see the boy
through an unseeing night
of mumbling helpless
incoherent confusion
next day his sight returned
and the boy spent his summer
days and nights
at the children's home
untoughened up perhaps
but unburdened more

Early one evening a psychiatrist recently appointed as a consultant to a children's home answered the telephone to hear, "We've got an emergency here. Bill Clay's out of his head. Doesn't even know where he is, and he's blind, too. He gets agitated, and tries to strike out at people. The houseparent took him to the pediatrician, but he said it was nothing physical and that he needed to see a psychiatrist. It all happened suddenly late this afternoon." It took the consultant about fifteen minutes to reach the children's home.

Bill, whom the consultant had not met before, was seventeen years old, about five feet, ten inches, in height, muscular, with long black hair. He was dressed in Levis and a half-unbuttoned blue shirt that hung out of his trousers. He was being half held and half restrained between two staff members, a man and a woman also unknown to the consultant. The three were sitting uneasily on the couch in the lobby of the administration building. The boy's face was flushed, his hair wet with perspiration and hanging in strings around his face. His voluntary muscles were tense and agitated. He repeatedly tried to free himself from the grasps of those trying to hold him. On breaking free, he would lurch forward, almost falling, or stumble unsteadily into a desk or into the wall. The continual muscular struggle was accompanied by vocal sounds, grunts, heavy sighs, and moaning, interspersed with angry, defiant-sounding "No's."

Such behavior could be related to many possible causative factors, and of first importance was an assessment of the functioning of the central nervous system. There was no obvious elevation of temperature. Deep and superficial reflexes were intact. There was no external evidence of trauma. The pupillary reflexes were normal, and fleeting glimpses of the optic fundi did not suggest any increase in intracranial pressure. There were no signs suggestive of toxicity from drugs.

This assessment of necessity was cursory because of Bill's general state of uncooperativeness, but it was sufficient partially to rule out some possible causes of the behavior.

On first seeing this boy, the consultant's first thought, on the basis of previous experiences with adolescents presenting a similar picture, was that the reaction was most likely one often referred to as a dissociative reaction.[1] Yet it was extremely important to try to rule out other possibilities, as any attempt to be of help had to be based on some rational plan.

The anxiety and fears of the four staff persons present were obvious and understandable; they had been through a very uneasy time in the past few hours with this young man. In an attempt to try to alleviate some of the group anxiety and thus develop a helpful plan for the boy, the consultant sought information that would help to reconstruct the chain of events leading up to the moment. All present had partial information, and each was responsive to particular questions and could elaborate at length on information sought. As the group anxiety began to subside, information was supplied more spontaneously and in greater detail.

In addition to involving the group in providing current information, the consultant suggested some activities that were helpful in dealing with the group anxiety. One person was asked to bring certain items needed in the examination. Another was requested to bring the boy's file and review his medical record for pertinent information, and the two attempting to restrain the boy between them on the couch were asked merely to guard against his suddenly getting up and lurching uncontrollably and to let him move about more freely on the couch.

As soon as the consultant was reasonably satisfied that the boy was in no immediate danger from any specific cause such as drugs, trauma, or infection, the others present were so informed. This itself was most reassuring to them. The examination continued slowly, as the boy's degree of cooperation would allow.

1. Dissociative reactions are believed to occur in an individual under great stress whose self is severely threatened. As a means of protection from the perceived danger, there is an alteration of consciousness and/or function of some part of the body. As a result, the danger in the current situation is dissociated from past memories of crises, emotional conflicts, and stressful life situations, all of which have actually contributed to the overwhelming anxiety of the present. Unable to resolve the overwhelming anxiety, automatic repression or inhibition occurs, resulting in symptoms such as amnesia, blindness, paralysis of one or more limbs, or loss of sensation over part of the body. Such symptoms may occur singly or in combination. The symptoms lessen the immediate anxiety, and although they do not help in the long run, the individual is temporarily more comfortable. Where the state of consciousness itself is altered, as in amnesia, the individual is often unable to recall anything that transpired during that time.

Over a period of an hour and a half, while the examination and information gathering continued unhurriedly, the group anxiety lowered. It was noticeable, too, that the boy rather gradually became more cooperative. He did not resist such procedures as examining his heart, checking reflexes, and taking his blood pressure. He did not respond to requests or directions, but the agitation diminished.

Although the information came in bits and pieces from various persons and sources, a rather remarkable story emerged. Several days prior to the occurrence of this episode the boy had gone, in the company of another boy from the home, to attend a survival training program, approximately a hundred miles distant. Bill had at first said that he would not attend this program; then, with some increasing pressure from staff, he had finally, but reluctantly, agreed to go. He had been silent on the trip to the remote site, though he had expressed disappointment that he had not been able to say good-bye to his girlfriend who would be leaving town while he was away.

The strong wish on the part of the staff for him to attend this program was based on the perception that Bill was becoming more and more dependent on his place in the institution. He had come to the children's home approximately two years before, and these two years were the longest period that he had lived in one location since his very early childhood. He was considered a quiet, cooperative, intelligent young man. He attended public school but had no outside involvement at school, or anywhere else, as far as was known. His visibility at the home was low, and he went about his business in a quiet manner, causing no problems.

The staff's concern about his dependency on the home was based on the knowledge that within two years he would be graduated from high school and, in accordance with the home's policy, would then move out into the world. No definite vocational or educational plan had been formulated thus far.

In the past the home had dealt with institutional dependency by programming adolescents into community activities, including the survival training program. Another plan that had worked fairly successfully over many years with a number of the boys was to have them move into an apartment and find summer employment off the campus for a summer or two before their final separation from the home.

Staff had discussed with Bill the wish that on his return from survival camp he would find a job and an apartment for the summer and return to campus before school began in the fall.

After three days at survival camp, Bill reported that he had a headache. The leaders urged that he continue, but he showed little motivation to do so; and as their urging continued he reported that the headache was more severe. Under these circumstances they felt that he should not be pushed further, and they called the director of the children's home to say that someone should come for this boy because of the headache and his unwillingness to continue in the activities.

Transportation was dispatched to the swamps, and Bill returned to the campus about the middle of the morning. By the time he reached the campus, the boy's complaints about his headache had subsided. Staff made the decision that morning that Bill should immediately begin looking for an apartment. Reasoning that Bill might feel he had failed in the survival venture, staff thought that it made sense to move him immediately into looking for an apartment prior to obtaining a summer job.

Again, the boy showed reluctance, but after some direct pressure from the director he had gone with a young woman staff member to look for an apartment. They left the campus before noon, going from one advertised apartment to another, searching for a place that was comfortable and yet reasonably priced. The home would underwrite the cost of the apartment to get the boy started; he was to take over payment as soon as a job was found. Bill and the staff member looked all afternoon but had no success in locating an apartment that was within the range of what the boy was likely to be able to pay.

Late in the afternoon, as they were driving along the boulevard with the boy at the wheel, he told the staff person that his headache was beginning again. They were en route to the children's home, and she told him that they would find some medicine on their return that would help him.

A few minutes later he told her with alarm in his voice that his vision was becoming blurred and that he was going to pull over so that she could drive the car. He did this, and they exchanged places.

Within minutes after this exchange, the boy became more apprehensive and told the staff person that he could not see at all. She was quite alarmed and told him that she would turn around and drive to the doctor's office immediately. She tried to talk with him to keep him calm on this leg of the journey but later reported that he became more anxious and his talk more disconnected as they approached the clinic that routinely took care of the medical needs of the children's home.

She was able to get him into the office without great difficulty. The pediatrician told them that this was not something that he could deal with and suggested that a psychiatrist should see the boy. As the staff person remembered it, there had been no physical examination. She returned to the car with the boy and drove as quickly as she could to the children's home. By the time they reached the home she was even more alarmed because Bill appeared to be completely incoherent and was becoming more agitated.

The background information contained in Bill's record was limited and sketched in meager fashion the previous significant experiences in his life. Apparently the data had been gathered rather quickly two years previously in another city in the state when his absences from school had been reported to the authorities and an investigation had been made by the Department of Social Services. At that time, he had been placed in a detention home while the plan was worked out for his entry into the children's home.

The information in the record indicated a nomadic life. At birth he had been taken from a hospital by a Mr. Clay, apparently not a relative of his. It was simply stated in the record that the baby was "given to Mr. Clay" with no information as to the circumstances or the reason for such an arrangement.

Bill lived with the Clays until about the age of five, at which time Mrs. Clay died. There was no information as to the kind of care he received and no information as to the cause or circumstances of the foster mother's death.

Soon after the death of the foster mother, Mr. Clay remarried, and the record indicated only that this was a very stormy marriage lasting a couple of years. The new Mrs. Clay apparently had several children of her own who came with her into this marriage.

The history did state that Mr. Clay had a lifelong problem with alcohol, that he was in ill health, and that he had been employed for brief periods of time in an assortment of odd jobs not requiring any particular amount of training or skill.

Mr. Clay kept the boy with him after the breakup of the second marriage and was the sole parent from the time Bill was about seven years old until he was nearly fifteen. The history also stated that Mr. Clay had moved frequently, going from one town to another in the state; and on at least one occasion he had moved to another state. Since his admission to the children's home, Bill had kept in touch with his foster father, who continued to move from one place to another. At least two or three times a year the boy would go to visit Mr. Clay, and he always returned in a saddened state, worried about his foster father's health or about the conditions under which he was living.

In the record, there was a letter the boy had written just prior to his admission to the children's home. He had visited the home on one occasion, having been brought by the caseworker assigned to him while he was in the detention home. On his return to the detention home, he had written a letter at the request of the intake social worker at the children's home, saying why he wanted to come there to live. This was a simple, straightforward statement expressing what are really the basic needs of any individual. The boy said that he needed a place to live; that he thought the children's home would provide him with food; that he needed to continue in school; and that the people he had met at the children's home on his visit seemed "like nice people." He added that for his part of the agreement he would expect to follow the rules, that he would do whatever tasks were assigned to him and would not cause any trouble. He ended his short letter with a plea that he be allowed to come to the children's home to live.

From the information in the record and the statements of the staff at the children's home, one would say that he had made a satisfactory entrance and adaptation. He had been well liked from the beginning by staff and the other children. With the exception of the infrequent visits to his foster father, he had remained very close to the campus.

Bill had attended public school during both of his years in the children's home and passed his grade each year. His record had not been outstanding, but he had not been in severe academic difficulty. For the most part he had received *C*s and *D*s with an occasional *B*. There had been no problems such as truancy or running away. It had been observed that he appeared to be a natural athlete in some intramural games on the campus but that he had no great interest in sports and had not participated in sports at his school.

Bill was described as a very quiet boy who appeared to be of average intelligence and who was quite sensitive to the moods and needs of others, both staff and children. At no time had he been willing to talk with his caseworker or other staff about his personal life or about his experiences prior to coming to the children's home. When asked questions about this, he would respond in a matter-of-fact way without any outward show of emotion or feelings. He always responded briefly, conveying the impression that he did not wish to talk about these experiences. He was described as "always holding his feelings within himself."

The boy had formed a close relationship with one other boy on the campus, his roommate, and they spent most of their time together. He was liked by other children and in his quiet way appeared to be one of the boys, "to whom others looked up." He was respected by staff also.

Bill's health had been good during the two years at the home, but the record indicated that he had experienced headaches from time to time. He had been seen by a physician who had diagnosed the attacks as migraine headache and had given him medicine to take at the onset of symptoms. There was no good description available of the pattern of the headaches.

The boy's agitation and uncooperativeness gradually began to subside as the physical and neurological examination continued, and the consultant began to speak directly to the boy, asking him to do particular neuromuscular maneuvers as a part of the neurological assessment. It became obvious that he was receiving and processing these spoken requests to some extent, as indicated by his attempts at compliance. The next step was to try to elicit some verbal response from him, and this came first in the form of a very soft yes or no. His state of consciousness expanded gradually, and he began to respond with simple statements. At one time he conveyed the need to go to the bathroom; however, he could not see and had to be led there. After this, his eyes were examined again and he responded to the penlight, saying that he could see the light but that everything was blurred. He could not identify the number of fingers or objects held before him. Vision improved over a matter of several minutes. By now, he was steadier on his feet.

Some definitive plan of care was needed. There seemed to be two choices: taking him to a hospital where he could be under continuous observation and care or having him remain at the children's home.

In favor of the hospital was the possibility of the return of symptoms; it would have been difficult to match the hospital's degree of observation in the cottage where he lived. There was only one houseparent on duty, and there were ten other children in the cottage. Also it was felt that the other children would be alarmed should he be returned to the cottage.

Against sending him to the hospital was the fact that he would be quartered in the psychiatric unit with many other patients in various states of disturbance. This would be a new and strange environment for him and would undoubtedly create additional anxieties for him. Also, all of the persons with whom he would come in contact there, even for a brief period of time, would be unknown to him. Further, there was the possibility that this plan might carry some stigma for him.

This temporary dilemma was resolved when the staff that was present, after discussion, devised another plan by which he could be cared for at the children's home. There was an apartment available upstairs in the administration building. The director called a number of other persons who were off duty and was quickly able to mobilize a sufficient number of persons to stay with the boy throughout the night.

Staff members selected were those who knew Bill at closest range. It was thought advisable to have two persons present at all times in the event that he should become agitated and need to be restrained. No one declined the request to spend time with him throughout the night. But everyone had to work next day—business had to go on as usual in caring for all of the other children in the home—so "watches" were set up throughout the night in two-hour blocks of time with a man and a woman always present.

This plan was designed without Bill's knowledge because the director did not know whether he would be able to locate enough persons to carry it out. However, with the director helping to take one shift, the schedule was arranged rather quickly. Then the alternatives were explained to the boy, who said that he wanted to go to his room in the cottage but that if he could not do that he would rather remain in the apartment than go to the hospital.

Appearing physically and emotionally exhausted, the boy was accompanied to the apartment where he went immediately to bed. He did not talk spontaneously but responded rationally to questions and to requests. One of the counselors prepared a light snack for him, which he ate sparingly.

Instructions were given about neurological signs and symptoms to watch for, and those who were to stay with him were advised to let him talk about anything that he wanted to talk about but not to press him for any information. One person was to remain in the room with him while the other stayed in the sitting room of the apartment, ready to help should there be any cause for alarm at any time throughout the night.

Around 9:30 P.M. the boy was dozing somewhat restlessly but was relatively calm, and the consultant left for home. A call to the apartment around midnight and again about 6:30 the next morning indicated that all had gone well during the night. The boy had slept intermittently, and during his periods of wakefulness he had talked spontaneously about topical matters around the campus. He slept until about midmorning and was then allowed to return to his cottage where the day staff was in position to be watchful for any change in his behavior.

He said that he had a slight headache but that his vision was all right. He spent a quiet day in the cottage watching television and reading. He did not talk much to anyone and made no reference to the events of the preceding day and night.

It was thought advisable to follow up these events with some interviews that would allow the boy to become involved in psychotherapy if he wished. He was seen twice by appointment during that week and was on time for his appointments. However, he did not talk freely and gave the impression of not wishing to be under any pressure to talk about what had happened. He did say that he was unable to recall anything from the time his vision became blurred until he awoke the following morning in the apartment, and he did not recall the consultant having been present.

During these sessions he talked in a rather general manner about life on the campus and about school. He spoke of plans to find a job for the summer months. The administration had withdrawn its plan for him to find an off-campus apartment for the summer, and he expressed relief about this.

Bill recalled that he objected to attending the survival program, though he had not been very vocal about it. At the time of the telling, he showed no particular emotion but said that he had been angry about being sent against his wishes. He said several times that he knew he could have completed the program if he had wanted to and that he would have done so if he had not developed the headache. The closest he came to saying anything about apprehension at the survival site was to mention that there were boys from all over the country and he did not know any of them. It may have been significant that he repeated in several ways that he could have completed the course if the headache had not developed.

He came for two more appointments at weekly intervals, each time saying as he left that he did not think he needed to talk about what had happened but that he would be back next week. Each time there was little show of emotion, more general talk, and careful avoidance of material related to the events already described.

At the third weekly appointment there was a decided change in his attitude. On this occasion Bill wanted to talk and promptly began to recall earlier years. He said that he could not recall too much about his first foster mother but that his impression was that she tried to take good care of him. He recalled her death, at which time he thought he was at home alone with her but was not sure about this. He remembered the fear and feeling of "being alone" he had experienced. He thought that even during those first five years the family had moved several times.

He recalled the two years after the remarriage of his foster father as a very unhappy experience. He talked about the second foster mother, how she had brought several small children of her own with her, and how he thought that she had never liked him. He knew that he did not like her. He spoke of her as treating him differently from her own children. He spoke of "unfair" punishment, including many whippings. Again, there was mention of moving around and never being settled. He recalled that he was glad when his foster father and the second foster mother separated. He said they had argued and fought the entire time they were together.

One theme that ran back as far as the boy could remember was that of his foster father's drinking. The foster father would start a job, drink too much, be dismissed, and when the grocery bills and rent bills mounted the family would move again. He recalled that from about his seventh to his fifteenth year they moved to many towns, sometimes to different houses in the same town, and on one occasion to another state. He said it seemed to him as a young child that they were always "running from something."

Another theme that emerged during this extended talk was that of hunger. Frequently there was no food in the house, and many times he went to school without food and would have none all day. He recalled stealing food from other children or a neighborhood grocery store.

Another unpleasant memory was that of always being different from other children, different not only in that he had no food but in that he had almost no clothes to wear. What he had were in rags, and he was often cold in the winter months. He recalled being laughed at and teased at school. An especially unpleasant memory was that of being told that he "smelled bad" by teachers and students. He said that this must have been true because his clothes were hardly ever washed. He recalled running away from school or leaving home for school and never arriving there. He would hang around the neighborhood or hide in an abandoned house in order to avoid going to school. He wondered how he had made any grades at all with his poor attendance record but thought that under other circumstances he would have done better. To compound all of this Bill spoke of his foster father's drinking and of many times when he thought the father was dying or had died.

Another matter that had always concerned him was the eternal question of why he had been given up by his natural parents. He had absolutely no information about them, and none ever had been given to him. He remembered being embarrassed and confused because his name was different from that of his foster father. During his first year at the children's home he had expressed a strong wish to have his last name changed to that of his foster father. Arrangements were made, and the change was executed through the courts. He said that, even though there were many aspects of his foster father's life that he did not like, Mr. Clay had given him a home of some kind and that he wanted to have the name of Clay rather than a last name whose origins he knew nothing about.

Bill talked about his headaches and said they had begun when he first started school. He was asked to give a detailed description of the headaches, and it was learned that the cranial distribution, the intensity, and the duration of these headaches did not fit the classical migraine headache pattern. Elaborating, Bill said that the headaches usually occurred when he was facing some kind of stress, such as having to go to school in unwashed, ragged clothes, being teased by children, being reprimanded by a teacher, or having to do something about which he was very uncomfortable.

He recalled being relieved when he was apprehended by the police for truancy just prior to the time that he came to the children's home. He said this was not the first time the police had picked him up for truancy but that there had been no follow-through before.

Near the end of the long interview (almost two hours) he shifted to more recent events and said that he had dreaded returning to the campus from the survival program because he was afraid that staff would be angry with him. This was in fact the case.

Then he talked about his uneasy feelings, mixed with anger, on the day that he and the young staff person were looking for an apartment. He was discouraged that an apartment had not been found that he could afford. At the same time, he said he did not want to be alone in an apartment away from the campus. He dreaded returning to the campus after not finding an apartment, because he felt that significant persons were annoyed about his not staying at survival camp. Bill still had no recall of events between the onset of the blurred vision in the afternoon and awaking the following morning in the campus apartment.

This extended statement by the boy was remarkable in that it differed so much from what he had been able to bring out at previous meetings. He was relaxed, eager to talk, and the information flowed spontaneously. Instead of the detached, guarded attitude he had shown earlier, he displayed a readiness to "tell my story," as he put it. His affect was appropriate for the content of his story; especially when he was talking about his earlier years, large tears welled up in his eyes and overflowed.

He ended the session by saying that he liked his dad and felt that he wanted to help him in the future. He had for a long time thought that maybe in some way he could be instrumental in helping his father to give up his dependence on alcohol, but that he now realized he could not do that. He doubted whether his foster father ever could or would stop drinking. Bill had harbored a plan to finish high school and return to live with and take care of Mr. Clay by finding a job in the town where his foster father lived. However, he said that more recently he had been thinking that he would finish high school, get some training that would equip him for some kind of trade, and help his foster father by providing financial support. He said that he had come to realize that he had his own life to live and that he needed to get on with that.

He made an appointment for the following week but canceled it before the consultant's return to the children's home that day. He told the secretary that he did not think he needed to see the psychiatrist any more but that if he did he would let her know.

Bill found a part-time summer job, and several times he came by the consultant's office "just to say hello" and to report that he was all right. There was a quality of trust in these subsequent brief encounters; he was always quite friendly and shook hands warmly.

Staff was of the opinion that Bill had had a satisfactory summer with no repetition of the kind of episode that has been described. He was thought to be in a cheerful frame of mind and gave no obvious indication of depression. He had an occasional headache that apparently did not amount to anything and did not keep him from performing whatever his duties were at the particular time.

There is no way that one can analyze material of this kind in retrospect and be altogether sure that the analysis is correct. However, many clues worth noting can be picked up from the material presented.

In the first place, considering all of the stressful experiences this boy had gone through, it appears on the surface to be remarkable that he had made so successful an overall adaptation. It was evident in the few talks the consultant had with him that he was very sensitive and perceptive. Although his sense of self-worth had fluctuated, he had developed strength of character and had done well to progress in school with some degree of success despite frequent and extended absences.

Although there is limited information about the first five years, we are told that he was placed with foster parents immediately after birth, so he had early affectional attachments. He could not recall much about his first foster mother, but one would assume that this must have been a satisfying relationship in view of his capacity for trust.

Then, one would speculate that after the death of his first foster mother he had experienced until the age of fifteen a degree of caring by the foster father. These years had been filled with such inconsistency, deprivation, and mobility, accompanied by embarrassment, hurt, and shame, that he had become to an extent an isolate. Although he gave the distinct impression of having the capacity for trust, this no doubt had been impaired by the vicissitudes he endured.

The period between the ages of five and fifteen has been described as one in which Bill must have functioned very marginally. Along this line, we have no data to suggest that he had ever experienced any degree of success in belonging to any group. One sees evidence of his search for identity when he talks about his embarrassment when he was young at having a name different from that of the father with whom he lived. This is later borne out by his wish to have his last name changed to that of the foster father, even though the boy was able to say that the foster father's life style and many of his personal qualities had caused him great anguish.

This boy's basic needs had been met by his living in the children's home for a couple of years, and even though he was liked by

children and staff he maintained an unwillingness or an inca-
pacity to become much involved with a group, either at the home
or in school. One would speculate that he had experienced such
painful emotions over a span of years that he was reluctant to risk
himself in relation to groups. His characteristic mode of relating
appeared to be one of calm on the surface and reluctance to become deeply involved on a feeling level with others, with the
possible exception of the roommate.

He disclosed that he was quite angry about being pressured into
attending the survival camp but that he did not give vent to his
feelings, verbally or otherwise, prior to reaching the camp. On the
basis of the above information, one can only speculate that he
probably had some real fear about risking himself in this situation
and that he was also threatened by the requirement for close,
small-group involvement in the survival tests ahead.

The headache that precipitated his return from camp may have
saved him from further participation in something of which he was
quite fearful. He disclosed that the headaches had been with him
intermittently as long as he could remember and that on many
occasions he had been able legitimately to leave school when the
headaches occurred; and he reported that they frequently occurred
under stress, such as embarrassment at being teased and criticized by others, pupils and teachers. The headache may indeed
have been some variant of a migraine headache, but the description he gave did not fit the classical description and it may have
been a "learned" mechanism of defense. At the time of the onset
of the dissociative reaction, he may indeed have felt threatened by
the angry reception he had anticipated on his return to the campus and also by the loneliness he would experience when he was
"thrown off the campus," as he viewed it. Why the episode occurred on the return trip to the campus is not clear. No apartment
had been found, and the threat of returning and facing the problems ahead may have been the last straw.

The disappearance of the symptoms over a period of several
hours probably could be related to his being returned to familiar
surroundings and kept in a quiet, reassuring atmosphere. This is a
general mode of approach in dissociative reactions, although various medications have been used at times. An additional factor in
his recovery of function may have been the slow and comprehen-

sive physical examination. From all indications, this boy was not processing auditory and visual stimuli but was responding, albeit negatively, to tactile and positional stimulation. (Many similar reactions have been observed in young airmen when given a physical examination after a period of stressful combat. They become organized again during the physical examination procedures. Unhurried touching and tactile stimulation, along with a quiet, reassuring verbal tone, may have been the immediate factors that helped to make it safe for the individual to begin to reorganize his personality. This is more than a casual observation, as a number of these individuals have later spoken about their subjective feelings of safety and of being protected by a thorough examination and the reassurance that goes along with such a detailed procedure.)

The small group of staff members involved in the emergency demonstrated their helpfulness. A number of them, relatively unknown to each other, came together in the face of an external threat and quickly became organized, accepting various leadership roles and carrying out in a highly cooperative manner the steps necessary to arrive at the immediate goal of helping this boy to reintegrate his personality. Without this cooperation, the psychiatrist's task would have been much more difficult and Bill's care less reassuring to him.

CHAPTER 5

Involving Parents in Therapy

The family hoped and prayed
he'd soon be fixed
and home with them again

THE FAMILY

On the interstate
One early morning
As cars whizzed by
In the April rain

They stood in a line
In stair-step sizes
A mother, a son
A daughter of six

Mother held a cookie tin
The boy a new baseball
And the daughter of six
A bouquet of flowers

Inside the car and warm
They said they'd hitched
All the way from Crozet
That day to see

Their son and brother
At the children's place
They missed him a lot
And hoped and prayed

He'd soon be fixed
And home with them
His father couldn't come
He had to plow his land

The problems of therapeutic work with parents of children in residential care are numerous. Nearly every children's center makes frequent mention, both in its policies and in its publicity, of work with parents or parent substitutes, but on closer inspection it often appears that there is more *talk* about working with parents than actual work with them. It is as though we are not quite orthodox in our efforts if we do not make frequent references to parents. The brochures and informational pamphlets always call attention to this phase of our work. It is important, and most of the time families are there, although they may not always function well. This is the core of the problem in trying to work with a total family to resolve the problems manifested by the child who is in group care.

There are in fact special circumstances in many of these families that make working with them especially difficult. In order to expend our efforts in ways and directions that are most likely to help, we need to recognize and keep in mind these special circumstances. Frank Lloyd Wright, the premier architect of his time, is credited with saying that form follows function. May that not be true also in our work with families? That is, the form or structure of our therapeutic efforts must be geared to a realistic assessment of, and respect for, the peculiar characteristics of a particular family.

Not all parents will, or can, work in individual, group, or family therapy, or whatever the structure of the modality in which we as "helpers" develop a certain comfort and expertise. Therapy, with a capital *T*, is not for everyone. Even when parents have voluntarily placed the child in a group-care facility and do not have to overcome the problems brought on by a forced removal from the home, these special circumstances can complicate our efforts.

Some of the special circumstances we need to be aware of are sociocultural, geographic, and psychological. As an example of the first, the socioeconomic and educational backgrounds of the parents may differ so greatly from those of the therapists that out of fear and anxiety parents do not involve themselves. This may be a matter of clothes, speech, or social interaction. Parents, despite therapists' efforts, may feel inferior and different. They may not understand the language used, for therapists may forget that to an extent they use a special language, however jargon-free they attempt to make it. Then, too, there is sometimes a problem of community stigma. Some parents do not wish the visibility in their neighborhood or community that may result from regular visits to the group residence setting. They do not want to advertise the fact that their child is in group care. Often they speak of the child as being away in "boarding school" and avoid embarrassment to themselves by not visiting. The neighbors probably know the truth, but the parents need to maintain the social pretense. This may be particularly important when the parents have admitted their child to an agency over the objections of other members of the extended family. They feel isolated from other family relationships, and to visit would be to renew the painful criticism of family.

Logistics come into play when children in group care come from a wide geographic area. The reality of transportation costs, money for food and lodging, and care of children left at home may be so overwhelming as to preclude any attempt at regular visits on the part of the parents. The loss of a day's wage may be crucial in an already overburdened household, even where distance is not involved. Some employers are most understanding, but others have no sympathy for the worker wishing to be absent on a regular basis for an undetermined, often prolonged period of time. Availability of appointment times at other than the usual working hours may help. Many places use evenings or weekend time for appointments.

Guilt about placing the child or about their inability to manage him or her themselves and doubts about their capabilities as parents are strong psychological factors. This may be reinforced by what happens at the center. Many times when a youngster is removed from home to a residential setting there may be rather prompt improvement in the behavioral difficulties that resulted in admission. To see staff members working effectively with the child, to see a happier, better-adjusted child, may serve to remind parents of their own inadequacies. On a nonverbal or even a verbal level some staff members may see themselves as better parents to the child than the real parents. They may begin to compete, each trying to be the "good parent" to the child. Parents may sense this attitude on the part of staff and withdraw or go so far as to remove the child from residence.

On the other hand, conflictual attitudes and behavior may have been of such dimensions and have persisted for so long that parents breathe a sigh of relief when the child has gone. After a time of respite, they may involve themselves in therapy or casework. But again they may not, or they may involve themselves only minimally. This is often a clue that they do not want the child back in their home. They may deny any recognition of improvement in the child and may be very critical, at a distance, of the agency, even though the child may be markedly improved.

We should be slow in taking the position that a family has little or no affectional attachment to the child, but the fact remains that there are many, many children who are not valued by families, judging from the sustained attitudes and behaviors exhibited. This is a very difficult situation for a child of any age, for almost universally it appears that the child has some parental attachments in fact or in fantasies that idealize parents. If this lack of care and interest, for whatever reason, continues, some other planning for the child's future must be made in conjoint effort with other responsible individuals and agencies.

There may also be discord within the family. One parent may have prevailed at a particular moment, which resulted in admission of the child, although the other parent may have objected bitterly. Even though on one level the objecting parent may be relieved that the child is away, this cannot be admitted. Instead, conflict between parents may intensify, with the objecting parent blocking family participation in therapy. At the same time, the objecting parent makes no move to return the child home; he or she may actually prevent it. Meanwhile, the number of actors in the family drama is reduced by the absence of the child, but the conflict between parents mounts.

Parents may be suspicious of the agency itself. In many instances families have had long and irregular associations and encounters with many agencies—social services, outpatient clinics, police, or courts. Sometimes high levels of animosity have been built up, and this attitude is readily transferred to the next agency. Such parents regard the child treatment agency as another in a long line of agencies viewed as interfering with and intruding into their lives. Many reasons are put forth for not keeping appointments, and it may be exceedingly difficult to engage the parents on behalf of their child.

Yet some kind of continuing relationship with the family (or family surrogate) is of utmost importance to a child. For many children with poor self-identity, tenuous attachments, and a poorly developed sense of time, admission to group care feels as if it is forever. There are accompanying feelings of rejection and abandonment, additional burdens generated by the separation that contribute to a superimposed depression along with whatever internal and external disturbances already exist.

Anyone associated with group care has seen the disappointment and accompanying emotions in a child when parents, social service workers, volunteers, or others do not show up at the appointed time. There must be windows through which the outside world is visible and lifelines of hope to significant persons and associations beyond the agency boundaries. Without these, there is lurking depression, helplessness, and hopelessness, and the matrix for steadily increasing dependency with its corollary of diminished autonomy, typified by the "institutional child" about whom so much has been written.

Therefore, continuing, uninterrupted effort needs to be made to involve parents, or other significant surrogates, in the care and treatment process. Many agencies have used novel methods indeed to help accomplish this result.

In one institution, for instance, coffee and refreshments were provided in a large room on visiting day. This was primarily a social occasion. Some staff attended briefly, and parents became acquainted with each other and with staff members in a relaxed, informal atmosphere. This kaffeeklatsch became a regular, continuing affair, with some parents deciding they wanted to be a part of it by bringing cakes, cookies, and other goodies.

Staff was of the definite opinion that the affair led to improved staff-parent interaction and eased parental apprehension about becoming involved. More parents participated regularly when the parents themselves took over part of the preparation of refreshments.

Another agency showed a series of movies on days when clusters of parents visited, with two staff members assuming responsibility for each series and being present at each showing. The movies were films on child growth and development. Parents were encouraged to attend but were under no pressure to discuss the content of the films. Generally, however, quite a bit of discussion evolved, with parents and the two staff members participating. Therapists reported that the films frequently led to considerable discussion in their sessions with parents, giving them a focus for exploring family relationships.

In another instance, every two or three months the arts and crafts work of the children was placed on exhibit for a day. All the children helped prepare for this event and arranged their exhibits in the various media. The exhibit was held during specific hours on the scheduled day, usually a Friday afternoon, when many parents came to take their children for weekend visits. Refreshments were served, often prepared in part by the children. Children poured punch or served other drinks and were responsible for guiding their parents or other visitors through the large exhibit. They also conducted staff members individually or in small groups through the tour. This event was very popular and provided a pleasant atmosphere for informal exchange among staff, parents, and children. At least twice a year staff and children mounted a joint arts and crafts show, and this, too, was popular with all concerned, again extending the common experience.

Similar events that have much the same impact are outdoor carnivals or country fairs and Christmas pageants in which all can join in fun and games that often have special meaning for the parents.

In some instances, action groups emerge from the associations formed by parents sharing such common experiences. These groups have been able to identify unmet needs of emotionally disturbed children and subsequently to influence legislators and other public and private officials to pass appropriate legislation or to fund more appropriately already established children's programs. Such groups are invaluable in extending and solidifying needed services for disturbed children. In addition, through the liaison established with professional persons there is already a level of communication that is devoid of the sometimes mutual mistrust between professionals and parents of disturbed children.

A traveling field unit, in addition to its value at intake or in follow-up activities, can also serve as a valuable link with parents in remote sections of the state, particularly where distances, economic level, and relative cultural isolation may have combined to prevent any regular or frequent visiting of parents to the residential agency. In the majority of such cases, one or more local agencies are already involved with the family and have been, in fact, instrumental in arranging for admission of the child. Members of one such unit met regularly with parents in a particular region of the state, most often in the offices of the public health clinic, social services, local mental health clinic, general hospital, or children's hospital.

In many instances when parents did not wish to come to the local setting to talk with staff from the residential agency, the public health nurse or social worker arranged for a home visit by a residential staff member or two in the company of the local person, who gave credibility to the visiting staff person, and there was never any rebuff. The local nurse or social worker was a gold mine of information about every aspect of living in that part of the state, providing informally the social, cultural, and health information a visitor could never glean alone. Thus, there was a reciprocal educational process in this relationship, as well as a climate that was most conducive to parent and interagency cooperation in attempting to help a given child. As time went on, some of these same parents in whose homes staff had visited were the persons who recommended the residential agency's services to other parents in the community. In some communities, once the local person had prepared the way by personal introductions, the field unit made regular home visits on each trip.

In some cases, when the parents simply could not make the long journey to the residential center, and where considerable parent work was thought advisable, a local agency representative worked with the parents regularly. When the field unit made its regular visit to that community it could consult with the local representative about the total situation and then both could meet with the parents. The face-to-face involvement of the two persons working with the family was most useful. Everyone concerned knew each other personally, a far more satisfactory situation than two therapists exchanging letters or telephone calls without ever meeting.

In some circumstances, parents will not come to the child agency, nor do they want the worker to visit their home. They will agree, however, to meet at a neutral site such as the public library, a park bench at noon when they are on their lunch hour, the town square, or some other place mutually agreed upon. An agency representative willing to meet a parent in this manner can often prepare the way for more direct therapeutic involvement of the parent later on.

It is not unusual for a parent to be in prison while a child is in group care. Sometimes, too, a parent is confined by chronic illness or disability in an extended-care facility. In these cases it is important for social workers to make regular visits to see the parent, often taking the child along, thus planning with the parent about the child's future and at the same time keeping the two in touch during a critical time for each.

In one such case two brothers were in a children's home, having been placed there after their mother abandoned them and their father went to prison for theft. The father was interested in the boys, and together they made realistic plans for being together again, with the boys and their social worker making regular visits to the prison.

Sometimes, when the available parent is confined to a hospital, regular visits by the agency representative and the child may influence some member of the extended family to provide support for the child after residential care is no longer necessary. At the very least, affectional ties with family may be strengthened.

When one or both parents and the child are living with either set of grandparents, there may be a special interlocking of dynamics that needs exploration. Sometimes this can be done in family therapy, but often it is not practical for all to come to the group-care setting. Here is another instance when home visits will provide additional insight. There may be very ambivalent and destructive relationships that are not solvable in a limited time or not subject to change at all. The child is often the pawn in the family's struggle and thus finds himself with two sets of parents, all figures in conflict with each other. The child's parents may also have a markedly dependent relationship to the grandparents and may have relinquished rearing of the child to them, while at the same time deeply resenting this usurpation of their rights and responsibilities. In still other cases the parents may abandon a child, though physically they are still present, and grandparents have to assume grandchild-rearing responsibilities against their wishes, while experiencing continuing disappointment and frustration with their own son or daughter.

These are complex and often deep-seated situations that sometimes deserve more investigation than is carried out. Extra time and effort often helps clarify what therapeutic routes are possible.

On the other hand, grandparents, under the most trying conditions, may prove to be the only family resource that can be mobilized in support of a child. The case of Jesse illustrates the helpfulness of a set of grandparents.

Jesse was a small eleven-year-old, quite bright but with low self-esteem and almost no friends among peers. He was very suspicious of others and had a whining, demanding approach to adults. It was obvious from his pinched, anxious face that he was a most unhappy child. During his early life, nurture and support had been uncertain. The boy's father was dead, and the mother was nomadic, her instability and undependability accentuated by excessive drinking. At times the child had been shifted to an aunt, and when she could no longer care for him, he was brought to the home of the aging, semiinvalid maternal grandparents. The mother disappeared, and there was no other extended family to provide a support system.

The grandparents tried to provide a home for him with some community support and some help from the woman who was their part-time housekeeper. Even so, Jesse became more disturbed and difficult to care for. His symptoms grew worse, and he began running away. With the assistance of a public health nurse, admission was arranged for him to a children's center nearly 200 miles away.

At the center, Jesse's progress was slow, but by the end of a year he had made much improvement. He developed many friendships with other children; his suspicious attitude gave way to trust; his face and entire appearance changed; and he was able to enjoy living. Meanwhile, the grandparents' health had grown worse, and there was no alternative placement available for him. With the public health nurse acting as liaison between the center and the grandparents, a plan was devised for him to go to a boarding school. The nurse made weekly visits to the grandparents and was in continual communication with the residential center, and the placement plan evolved through careful, coordinated work. Fortunately, the grandparents had modest funds and were able to support the boy financially in the school. The boarding school selected was church related, and each small-group living unit for younger children had a married faculty couple as houseparents.

This plan worked out quite well for Jesse. He maintained his improvement and thrived on the nurture provided in the school setting. School breaks and vacations were spent with the grandparents or in summer camp. Jesse finished high school and then returned to the grandparents' home. From there he commuted to a nearby college, giving much help and comfort to the grandparents in their last years.

In this example, the goodwill of caring but handicapped elderly persons was utilized in the long process of helping a severely emotionally disturbed child. It is a good demonstration of an effective interagency effort where the child's treatment agency was only indirectly involved with the grandparents.

Although full-time family placement was not possible because of the physical condition of the elderly grandparents, they were able to serve as part-time family and to help provide a more secure future for Jesse. This arrangement provided family continuity for Jesse, and later on he in turn gained satisfaction from being able to help the grandparents.

In other circumstances, parents may have too many "therapeutic" engagements. One example is that of an eleven-year-old boy admitted to a residential care agency after a long history of explosive outbursts, depression, threats at self-harm, constant conflict with peers, arguments with his stepmother, poor school performance, and truancy. He had lived with his father and stepmother for a time and then had been sent to live with mother and stepfather in another part of the country. His problem behavior continued in the new location, and he was then admitted for residential care.

Almost before she knew it, the young caseworker assigned to work with the family found herself in the middle of a most complicated and frustrating situation. The mother was seeing a psychologist once a week; an older daughter and a younger son were seeing the same psychologist for individual therapy once a week; the mother and stepfather were seeing both a marriage counselor and the agency caseworker once a week; and sometimes the daughter and younger son were members of this group. None of these therapists was in communication with any other, and there were conflicting opinions everywhere.

The agency caseworker and the boy's therapist discussed the matter and decided that it might be less confusing if the case-worker confined her work at that time to focusing on the boy's problems and on the parents' role in relation to the boy. This may have been an artificial narrowing of the focus, but it clarified the therapeutic efforts of the child-care agency.

After several months the other therapy sessions were discontinued by the parents and the child-care agency's work expanded to include efforts to be of assistance in some of the marital problems. The boy made much progress and was able to return to live with his mother and stepfather in less than a year after his admission.

When parents appear to be distant or uninvolved, the distance may be geographic or emotional. In either case there is frequently a question as to whether the parents wish the child to return to live with them. The placement of the child in residential group care appears to carry the message, "We can't live with this child but want you to take him or her and see what you can do. Meanwhile, we'll go about our business." Contained in the message is the idea that parents will permit only minimal participation for themselves, mainly restricted to providing financial support for the child's care. This attitude may not be apparent at first but quickly comes to the fore, especially when parents are pressed for involvement.

Such an attitude may be sufficient reason for an agency to decline admission or to discharge early. However, before any precipitous action is taken, the matter should be carefully considered. It may be possible to provide much direct help for the child and indirectly to help the parents. For instance, Jane was a six-year-old, partially sighted girl, the youngest child of a mother who died in a severe depression soon after the child's birth. The children at first were cared for by a woman who lived full-time in the household. The father, a successful and highly respected businessman, remarried when Jane was about three. The stepmother had three children of her own.

The new union was fraught with difficulty from the beginning, with most of the trouble focusing around Jane, who resented the dismissal of the child-caring person and the arrival of the new mother. There was no indication of mutual attachment between stepmother and child. The child was negativistic, destructive, beset by nightmares, and mistrustful of adults by the time of her admission to a treatment center. Repeated attempts at control by the parents had included whippings, isolation in a locked room, and placement in day-care settings. The child also had been in play therapy with a psychiatrist for a year, although parents had declined any regular and sustained participation in therapy.

During two years at the center, the child, though still troubled, made steady progress in trusting adults and socializing with other children. In fact, the early disturbing behavior largely disappeared. But each visit home for a weekend—and visits were very far apart—resulted in marked regression with a slow return to improved functioning. Eventually, on those occasions when the parents permitted a home visit, the child would become so anxious that the visit had to be delayed, and in some instances the weekend visit would terminate with the parents returning the girl early. Later the girl was able to say she did not want to visit but she grieved at not seeing her siblings. With no visits, the child's condition improved, and staff agreed that some plan had to be made for her future.

During these two years the parents had refused to be involved, and when pressed to come to the center to talk about the child's future they would cancel out at the last minute. It was only when told that the child was to be discharged by a certain date that they reluctantly entered the picture.

That the child could not come home was definitely the stepmother's position. Though obviously troubled, the father did not protest. Yet both agreed that "We'll never give the child up for adoption or foster home care." Jane herself said she wanted to live with a family.

Instead, a children's home was found in another city where the child could stay, if necessary, until she completed high school. The social worker assigned to the case transported Jane to this children's home for the assessment and took her there when she was admitted. The girl continued to do well and attended public school. Even though parents were less involved than the children's home wished—and less than they had promised—they were much more involved than they had been in the first residential center. Home visits became slightly more frequent and lasted for longer periods of time, and the girl was taken on family vacations for the first time.

No one really knows very much about the family dynamics. The first residential center, in the family's home town, might have posed a threat to the parents' social status had they become involved to any extent. The stepmother's attitude might have posed a threat to the marriage and to the entire family if the father had insisted that the daughter come home to stay. Still further, Jane's problems may have been a painful reminder of the prolonged problems of the natural mother before her death. These ideas, however, are speculation. At any rate, the girl has made progress, and perhaps the family has also. The outcome, thus far, might have been somewhat different if the first agency had taken a more rigid and aggressive approach with parents in the beginning or during the course of treatment.

Dane was a boy of ten who, along with a sister two years younger, was adopted by a childless family when he was six.

It appeared that war was declared on the day of adoption. Dane said that he did not understand why a strange family came and suddenly took them to be their children. He had liked the foster parents where they had lived as long as he could remember. Apparently, the placement there took place right after the sister's birth, though details, including adjustment in the foster family, were unavailable.

Dane said he tried to do everything possible in the adoptive home to get himself sent back to the foster home. The sister apparently made a satisfactory adjustment, and the boy described her as obedient. A critical piece of information, never elaborated, was that the family had wanted a single adoption, that of a girl. But they had taken both children at the urging of the social service agency.

Negativism at home, temper outbursts, pouting, lack of affection, and general defiance resulted in Dane's admission to residential care. He had been expelled from several schools in the community where he broke windows, cursed, fought, hit teachers, and performed poorly and erratically in academic work.

This continuing behavior was the reason the parents had entered him in weekly psychotherapy at a university outpatient clinic. The parents had withdrawn him when the clinic insisted that they must be involved in the treatment. Next he had been admitted to another university child psychiatry inpatient program. But when the staff there also requested that parents be involved in regular casework, they had again withdrawn the child in anger and indignation. After a few months at home where behavior worsened and there was talk of "turning the boy back to the state," the parents sought admission for him to a children's residential facility three states and several hundred miles from home.

The great distance precluded weekly visits, but the parents agreed to one visit per month. Assessment of the boy led staff to believe that they might help the child even with this visitation schedule in effect, and he was admitted. He stayed in residence one year. The parents visited a total of three times, and the boy had three visits home, either riding a bus or flying.

The early months in residence were so stormy that several times staff considered discharge. Parents were extremely critical of the agency from a distance, going into tirades on the telephone and writing long, vituperative letters. Several times, especially after visiting Dane, they threatened to withdraw the boy because of "staff ineptness and inadequacy of program."

Nevertheless, Dane stayed and his behavior and attitudes began to change for the better. He became less combative, worked hard in psychotherapy, gradually developed friendships, and made rapid progress in school. He took great pride in the fact that he rode a bus and functioned adequately in public school for six weeks before leaving. There came a time when his improved behavior was sustained enough in all areas that both he and the staff thought about discharge. The parents were noncommittal at first, then denied that he "could be that much improved."

"But they told me if I changed enough I could come back. I have changed, and they ought to give me a chance. I'll try my best," he said again and again. It did not work out that way. They did not take him back but instead arranged admission to a children's home not very far from where they lived. He could visit home, they explained, but they were not ready for him to return.

Dane's expressed wish was that he could get along all right in the children's home and that they would change their minds. "I understand a lot more now," he said.

He has done well in the children's home and has kept in touch with some of the staff in the residential center by letter and occasional telephone calls. But three years later he has not returned home to live, even though visits there are no longer so conflict-laden. He still has a place called "home," though, and as he says, "that's something."

The staff in the residential agency was well aware that the parents were not likely to involve themselves, based on the referral information from other agencies. The very distance between the parents' home and the residential center, when there were excellent therapeutic programs close at hand, would have suggested this.

In neither of the above examples do we know much about the determinants of parental attitudes. In each case parents chose not to "give up" the child. Both children improved greatly, though neither lives at home. Perhaps that would have been possible had the parents cooperated more wholeheartedly. But the children are being cared for and have made a place for themselves in continued group care. To have demanded more direct parental involvement in either case would probably have resulted in the child being removed from needed treatment.

There is always hope that the parents may shift their positions and attitudes as change occurs in their child, and many times this is exactly what happens. The next case will illustrate a case of this kind.

Jerry, a ten-year-old, was adopted by a childless couple when he was five. Two years later a child was born to the parents. At the time of referral to the children's agency the parents said they had experienced difficulty with the adopted son quite early. At first he had been somewhat mistrusting but gradually became more affectionate. However, when the natural son was born, Jerry became negativistic and had repeated outbursts of anger. The parents said he had always been extremely rough with the natural son and many times had attempted to hurt him by pinching or hitting. School had been a big problem, both parents repeating that they were sure he was retarded because he would not listen to anyone and could not learn anything. The boy had been in special classes at school and had been sent for counseling with a psychologist for several months.

At the time of Jerry's admission to the children's treatment home, the attitude of both parents was significant. All the information focused on the problems of the child; there was very limited direct information about the adoptive parents. They had not been involved in counseling with the psychologist and had insisted that all the problems were in the adoptive boy.

Although both parents agreed to come to the children's home regularly for psychiatric casework, this did not happen. The father did not come, even once, saying that his work was too demanding. The mother came a few times in the boy's early months in residence, and the father called on the telephone several times. On one of her sporadic and brief visits the mother indicated that they had decided they could not take the boy back to live with them when he left the center.

Meanwhile, Jerry was making progress: it was obvious that he could learn academically; his social behavior was improving, and his negativistic attitude steadily declining. He was liked by staff and children and obviously was enjoying life in the group setting.

At the social worker's insistence, the mother returned several weeks later, and this session was different from the others. She began immediately to speak of her feelings about her marriage, making several statements about how unfair she and her husband had been to Jerry since their natural child was born. They had focused attention on the natural child and had viewed Jerry as an imperfect intruder. She recognized on this visit the many positive changes in Jerry's behavior and even showed some affection for the boy when visiting with him.

After this visit, the parents decided to arrange therapy for themselves closer to home, but in addition the mother continued to come regularly to the residential center for her appointments there. The parents began to allow regular visits for Jerry at home, reporting that the visits were becoming more satisfactory. Although the father never came to the center, his attitude was markedly altered; and the mother described with pleasure their gratifying activities with Jerry on the home visits.

After nearly a year in residence, Jerry returned home to live, and follow-up a year later indicated that he was doing well and that the family was functioning more harmoniously than it had in years.

The child residential agency was never privy to the details of the long-standing marital conflict, but the beneficial effects of the parents' therapy were obvious. The turn of events could not have been predicted, but this case illustrates the importance of separation of child and family in some instances while feelings and attitudes are sorted out. It further demonstrates the importance of perseverance with families of children in group care.

Although it would be desirable for parents to be involved in working on their problems at the center where their child is in treatment, this is not always possible. For Jerry's family the arrangement described worked satisfactorily. Sometimes, though, referral of parents to outside sources of help is indicated—when a child center staff does not possess the necessary therapeutic skills, for example. There are times when a staff must face its own shortcomings. Also, some parents may require more intensive therapeutic involvement than a child center can provide. Therapeutic time available and distance of parents from the child center often are crucial factors.

The life circumstances are many and varied under which children come into residential care. Ideally, one would wish for two parents to be regularly involved in the caring and treatment process. But life is not ideal. Recognition of the different circumstances of each parent or parent surrogate is important. There are multiple determinants of parental cooperation with the residential agency, and a number of these have been mentioned.

In the cases briefly described, it appeared to be the better judgment to try to be of help to the children at a critical time and to exercise a degree of restraint regarding the personal equations of the parents. Working with situations of this kind is indeed a strenuous exercise in restraint and patience on the part of residential staff, but both are qualities worth cultivating. Children and parents may be helped, even though the outcome may not be always what we would consider ideal. For residential staff a certain mobility of mind and body is helpful in involving parents: mobility of mind for finding imaginative means of involving parents in a manner meaningful to them and potentially helpful to their child; mobility of body for moving beyond the boundaries of the residential agency. Out of these efforts may develop a therapeutic alliance.

PART II

Essays on Children's Problems

CHAPTER 6

Some Critical Events in Childhood

Playing at serious things

PHOBIA

Except for the expressions
of pain and agony
written on his moist face
you'd have thought for sure
the young boy was playing

In a way he was
playing at serious things
holding back the swollen dam
keeping the volcano from blowing
the world from coming to an end
his parents from dying

By touching three times
circling the table five
jumping the doorsill seven
washing his hands nine
but it was driven work
until he dropped exhausted.

Life is a continuum of experiences, many of them pleasant and benign. Others are critical events that threaten our being, physically, mentally, and socially. Many of these threatening experiences are inevitable, and how we weather them is important in relation to our future well-being. A particular critical event may leave one person devastated and fearful, whereas another person may recover from a similar experience without handicapping impediments.

Many people believe that critical events, if properly mastered, will serve as an immunizing factor in coping with future troubling experiences. This analogy may be built on the knowledge that certain diseases elicit an antibody response in the body, thus conveying protection from exposure to the disease-producing agent in the future. Further, introducing the causative agent in an altered or weakened form into the body in a time of health will stimulate the formation of antibodies. These antibodies will convey protection, without the person having to experience the disease in its more active state. A number of diseases, including measles, mumps, whooping cough, poliomyelitis, and diphtheria, are averted in this manner.

The idea of a kind of psychological immunization for children suggests that we as adults can help a child weather critical events in a manner that will enable that child to learn through one threatening experience more effective ways of coping when the next crisis occurs. In effect, we help that child learn to put events into perspective, thus strengthening the child's ego. We enlarge his reservoir of abilities to solve problems. There are ways to deal with catastrophic occurrences so that we can still go on. The memory of previous experiences enables us to anticipate future critical events so that when such events come we are somewhat prepared for them. Thus, we have a continuing knowledge of how to function in a less helpless, less overwhelmed manner.

Anyone who observes children closely over an extended period of time has certain impressions about psychological experiences in childhood that enhance or hinder a child's development. Among these are the things children fear.

Certain basic fears are common to all children once they are old enough to comprehend at all. They fear loss of love from persons important to them, they fear abandonment, and they fear physical harm. These basic themes recur in nearly every critical event that threatens a child.

When thinking about critical events we should keep in mind the ego mechanisms of defense that the personality uses to protect itself. These defense mechanisms are necessary, and everyone uses them to an extent every day. But in exaggerated form they are clues to the level of stress. A partial list includes denial, regression, sublimation, projection, substitution, displacement, reaction formation, and identification with the aggressor.

When a child is ill for a period of time a great many shifts and changes occur in both parents and child that need to be watched closely. Some children will react by becoming excessively passive, "leaning on" his or her parents and accepting fully their anxious care. Such a reaction can be prolonged much past the expected period of convalescence, with the child remaining in a more or less regressed state to the detriment of effective functioning. Certainly most parents are motivated by love in their concern for an ill child, but even those parents may need to be reminded that the child has improved and that it would be much healthier for all concerned if he were expected, or allowed, to do more things for himself.

On the other hand, some children have strong defenses against being passive and leaning on others; and even in the face of an illness requiring extensive nursing care they cannot accept it. These children show unusual stubbornness, obstinacy, and recalcitrant behavior, which may interfere with their recovery.

Some of us can recall rheumatic fever patients who become emotional invalids. Conversely, some children with rheumatic fever cannot tolerate inactivity and rest and tear around at dragster speed in an attempt to deal with anxiety about being passive and less independent.

Fears and anxieties surrounding a child's hospitalization are many and are experienced by both parents and child. We have attended to these discomforts more effectively in recent years by taking time for more detailed explanation of what will happen, sometimes arranging a previsit to the hospital, allowing parents to be with the child before surgery and soon after recovery and to make frequent visits while the child is in the hospital. All of these maneuvers have helped to lessen a child's separation anxiety, fears of abandonment, and fears of physical harm. Parents, too, have been comforted.

Yet we continually see children in states of great anxiety and agitation about their illnesses and operations. It is not surprising they should have such feelings. As adults we have the same ones, and we should be in better position to accept realities than children. They have not lived as long, they do not have past experiences to measure the present by, and hence they are more prone to frightening fantasies than adults.

A boy of twelve years went to a local hospital for an inguinal hernia repair. The surgery was uneventful, but the boy became quite anxious, restless, and somewhat disorganized in his thinking. One might have guessed that a boy just entering into puberty would have been concerned about his approaching manhood, but it was necessary for the house officer to sit with the boy, talk with him about many things, and listen carefully before the boy revealed his fantasy that something had been done during surgery that would alter the eventual functioning of his genitalia. In his fantasy he had been castrated.

Perhaps more helpful preparation could have been made prior to the surgery; it should have been attempted. In any event, one needs to be alert to this kind of possibility. Some brief discussion with the child ahead of time can often prevent such anxiety reactions, which can become chronic if not relieved. It is not sufficient for the doctor or social worker simply to explain what will happen. He must listen to the child's questions and try to help him clarify what the operation is about. This is a method of premastering anxiety. We see such attempts in younger children when they play doctor or nurse both before and after a hospital or surgical experience.

Children (like adults) are frightened by the idea of dying; and with the threat of a serious illness their private world may be completely occupied with such thoughts. It is most comforting if with considerable conviction we can reassure them that they will be all right. For the child with a probable fatal illness, however, the emotional climate surrounding his care is altered. The adults around him, parents and professionals alike, are affected by this. We are anxious, even angry inside that such has to be the fate of this person we love. But care must go on, and we often deal with our own feelings, as adults, by suppression, repression and denial, and avoidance.

The child senses this, and what life there is for him becomes extremely difficult. Those who care for children with leukemia, for example, often say that a particular child is greatly relieved when someone "gives him permission" to talk about these dreadful feelings that have been locked in his private world. Many people have made the observation that the child senses the gravity of the situation from the adults around but will not express his or her thoughts openly and directly; instead, the child waits for the adults to show a willingness to listen to these serious concerns. When such opportunities occur, these children frequently become more relaxed, less withdrawn, less obstinate, more cooperative in allowing procedures and taking medications, and happier in general.

Several years ago, when kidney transplant operations were relatively new, an attractive twelve-year-old girl, who had had such an operation, was behaving in anything but an attractive way. She moved around the hospital's transplant unit, complicating nursing procedures with other patients. She was quarrelsome and argumentative, frequently whined and cried, was often uncooperative with her own procedures, and was a general nuisance.

She had previously rejected two transplants but had been doing quite well for nearly a year with one of her father's kidneys. Soon after this latest transplant, the father left the family and his whereabouts were uncertain. There were other children in the family, and the mother was not having an easy time. To make matters more difficult, the child had developed a severe hearing loss during her prolonged illness, and it was hard to converse with her unless one took plenty of time.

A consultation request asked for assistance in "managing her," and this was sorely needed. The child, given an opportunity, was eager to talk about her illness and her life situation. She was afraid she would die but had never talked about it. Whenever she experienced a strange bodily sensation—a chilly feeling, unsteadiness, an ache or pain—she would be panic stricken and have to return to the hospital. She felt that something dreadful was happening inside, that she might be going into a coma, that her body was rejecting the latest kidney. She could not understand why her father had abandoned the family. Was it because of her? Didn't he love her? These and many other emotion-laden questions were constantly in this child's mind.

The emotional climate on the unit where she had spent so much time and received so much treatment, and to which she had to return periodically, deserves some comment. Patients received much attention and excellent care by a highly specialized and capable staff. Yet, a visitor to the unit would notice the cheerful atmosphere and a pervading attitude almost of gaiety. This was a unit where crisis was the order of the day and where the balance of life for many patients tottered precariously from week to week. It might be suggested that the staff, in order to live and work with its own anxieties, had to adopt cheerful attitudes for its own emotional economy. But beneath this protective surface attitude was always the threat of death and dying, suffering and pain. The little girl, during her series of interviews, talked about this and said, "I think everybody is real worried and afraid, and I am too; but nobody will talk with me about these things."

She was much relieved to be able to express her concerns, worries, and fears and became a considerably happier girl despite her difficult circumstances. These talks enabled her to ruminate less, to be less preoccupied with morbid thoughts, and to use her energy more productively. She got along better in school, was able to apply herself to the tasks at hand and gain satisfaction in her own daily accomplishments. This is not to say that she had no more worries; she obviously had many, but it was a definite turning point in her internal life when she was able to face more realistically a most difficult situation.

Prolonged illness of a parent may also test the emotional strength of a child, and the reactions to such an illness can be harmful. Children may be quietly curious about an illness and confused on hearing a diagnosis, but they may be reluctant to seek out more detailed information until someone provides an opportunity for them to do so. In prolonged illness the security of the child may be threatened by loss of economic support due to the parent's inability to work; but just as important to the child may be the loss of emotional support and nurture, which the ill parent is unable to provide. Then, too, one sees from time to time a child who is very closely identified with the parent who is ill and who develops various complaints of a psychosomatic nature. It is not unusual in a household that includes a chronically ill grandmother, for example, who is the matriarch of the family to see a child identify with her and develop a variety of complaints.

Occasionally, when a parent is ill, the child develops a sense of guilt about the illness, feeling that he or she had something to do with it, and suffers interminably in silence.

Paul's father underwent major brain surgery and had many months of terminal illness during which time he was kept at home. Paul's mother did the best she could under very adverse circumstances, but she seemed unaware of the suffering that Paul was experiencing. Absolute quiet had to be maintained in the house as the father was extremely irritable and suffered much pain. Paul was an active seven-year-old, and his mother had to reprimand him, sometimes whipping him, ejecting him from the house whenever he made any noise, and telling him that he was making his father worse. Day after day of this resulted in Paul's feeling more and more guilty and in his staying out of the house most of the time. He scurried around the neighborhood from one place to the other in a state of driven activity. Neighbors at first felt sympathy for him but soon were unable to tolerate his excessive dependence; he was both subtly and openly rejected. Beneath this state of excitability was real depression. The result was a nearly successful attempt at suicide by hanging.

Death is a difficult concept for children, and those who have studied children's reactions to it are of the opinion that it is somewhere along toward ten or twelve years of age before a child gradually takes in the concept that death is something that happens to everybody eventually. The quite young child may view death as reversible and think that someone "has gone away" and will return. This idea is often reinforced when parents and neighbors speak of someone who has died as having "gone to sleep," "gone on a trip," "gone away for a visit," or "gone to heaven." The child of five or six may believe that death is something that happens to other people but never to himself.

One can therefore anticipate many different reactions to death, depending on the age of the child, the circumstances under which the loss of a parent or relative occurred, and the child's earlier experiences. At around the age of four, five, and six, it is not uncommon for a child to feel a great amount of guilt when a parent of the same sex dies. These are the years when children are struggling with their identity formation and when they sometimes feel an intense rivalry with the parent of the same sex for the affection of the other parent. A little boy may be very angry with his father and may "wish he would go away." Then, when the parent has gone away on a business trip and an accident or sudden illness results in death, the child, who is not far removed from the magical omnipotence of the wish being the same as the deed, may feel totally responsible for something of which he was in no way the cause. Considerable help may be required for this child to understand that anger does not kill and that the wish is not the same as the deed.

When the loss of a parent does occur in these earlier years, it makes for a trying situation for all concerned. The economy of the household may be devastated. Also, the remaining parent, in his or her own grief and loneliness, may unconsciously seek gratification from the child for his or her own need for affection to a pathological degree. It does seem to be more difficult psychologically for the young child when the lost parent is of the same sex. For one thing, the child is left without a suitable model with whom to identify, and some very intense and often unhealthy relationships may develop between the child and the remaining parent. The little girl cannot be the "woman of the house," and the little boy cannot be the "man of the house."

It is not uncommon for the child, after the death of a parent of the same sex, to share the bedroom or bed of the parent of the opposite sex. Usually, it is the young boy who is sharing the bed with his mother. In many instances, the boy is as old as thirteen or fourteen. This situation is too emotion-laden and too much for the developing ego to tolerate.

Another critical event in a child's life may be the parents' separation or divorce. In the charged atmosphere leading up to this event, it is often difficult for parents to be reasonable and rational in their attitudes toward each other. They may both love the children, but usually the children are to an extent onlookers from the sidelines without sufficient emotional support. Their reactions will vary, and some children may feel an excessive amount of guilt, believing that they are the cause of the breakup of the marriage. If one thinks about it, this would not be an unreasonable reaction when either parent may displace angry feelings toward the spouse onto the children.

There is always the question of loyalty, and regardless of how shabbily children may have been treated by either parent they will still have some affection for that parent or feel entitled to some affection from him or her. It is a heavy burden for the child to be expected to renounce one parent completely for the other, and it can result in a great deal of guilt, confusion, and mistrust of other adults.

A really difficult problem occurs when a child is brought into court to testify against a parent. Fortunately, this practice is less common than it was. It may be a shattering emotional experience for a child, and it is almost always desirable for a child's statement to be made in the quiet of an office where he will not be subjected to the often histrionic, angry, charged atmosphere of the court-room.

The continual harangue of threats of divorce over months or years can reduce a child to a stressful state. Sally was eleven, with basically attractive features but an anxious, fearful expression on her young face and a large bruise on her left arm. Her mother and real father were divorced, and Sally lived with her mother and stepfather, the second marriage having taken place when Sally was five or six. What was the trouble? She worried all the time, did poorly in school work, had few friends, was argumentative and hostile toward other students. What did she worry about? For one thing, she worried abut her three brothers who lived with aged grandparents in a distant county. Then, too, she could not sleep because her mother and stepfather argued and fought in the night, threatening divorce, and Sally was afraid that her stepfather would kill her mother. Sometimes she went to their room to try to stop the fighting, but when she did the stepfather beat her. She was afraid he would come to her room and attack her there. What would happen to her if the parents separated? Would anyone take care of her?

Sally is a pathetic little girl who, if this situation continues, has little chance for healthy development. She is a prime candidate for leaving home early and entering into an impulsive marriage of her own. In so many life situations of this kind, it seems that "the apple doesn't fall far from the tree."

Our population is a mobile one, with a large segment of any community changing its place of residence each year. It is a tribute to the strengths of children and their families that such moves occur with such frequency and that adjustments are made without more major upsets occurring. Nevertheless, upsets do occur. Children grieve for their old friends and familiar surroundings to the extent that it interferes with their adaptation. It is generally difficult for adolescents to move, especially when one considers the importance of the peer group for adolescents and the importance of maintaining friendships. On the positive side is the fact that the young adolescent is old enough to understand the reasons for the move, to go through part of the grieving ahead of time, and to establish some means of staying in touch with old friends until new ones come along to fill the void. This they do by letter, telephone, and occasional visits back to the former place while they make the emotional shift necessary to go on.

It is not always so with younger children, and especially the preschool child who can become quite upset and confused when boundaries are suddenly shifted. If parents are aware of the importance of that which is familiar to a young child, they can devise many ways to make a move easier. Even so, in a children's psychiatric setting we are consulted frequently about a younger child whose family has moved. The child is extremely restless, has difficulty sleeping, has regressed to frequent temper tantrums and bed-wetting, and may even run away in his or her confusion to try to find something familiar.

Young children are subject to many kinds of deprivation. The word does not refer only to deprivation of physical needs. In fact, if emotional support is supplied by parents, a child can withstand much material deprivation.

In a children's clinic one is impressed by the number of children referred who have a variety of problems—restlessness, hyperactivity, apparent inability to learn academically, antisocial behavior, such as repeated stealing, running away, and cruelty to animals and other children. In many of these instances, a common theme is a very shaky infancy and early childhood. Perhaps the mother has to work, and the children when very young have a wide variety of mother figures to care, or not care, for them. Their histories frequently disclose inconsistency and inconstancy of parenting in the early years. (On the other hand, young mothers who have children while they are in midadolescence themselves and who have not reached a level of maturity where they are able to nurture an infant might be wiser to work and to try to provide a substitute mother who can give consistent love and care in the child's early years, when these things are so important.)

Many of these children have a history of a broken home with no suitable substitute for the absent father or mother, and because of this deprivation their psychological development has been malformed. There are additional problems if a parent is psychotic, psychopathic, or a chronic alcoholic. In some of these instances the children suffer great ego and superego deficits in their psychological development, and once they are past preschool years any kind of substitution or replacement attempt becomes increasingly less likely to yield an evenly and effectively functioning individual.

The separation that must take place when a child goes to school is a critical time, and it is a step that must be mastered if the child is to move ahead in his development. Fortunately, nursery schools and elementary schools are becoming more aware of the normal ties existing between mother and young child and are trying to make the separation easier. For instance, the teacher may visit in the home before a child enters school; mother and child may visit the school and the classroom setting prior to the opening of school so that the child can begin to become familiar with a widening world; the mother may go with the child to school the first few days and may remain nearby if there appears to be any marked anxiety about separating. When the teacher sees a particular child becoming anxious, she may signal the mother to enter the classroom and remain for a while. In this way the transition is generally made without too much turmoil. The buildup of anxiety and panic in an immature ego is averted and problems avoided later on. In instances of illness when a younger child has had to be out of school for a while, these reassurances may have to be repeated while the child again makes the transition from the home to the school.

Many other matters of an urgent nature deserve attention. Among these are the child with distorted body image as a result of accident, surgery, or anomaly; the child who has experienced excessive parental interference in his development and has not been trusted enough to be allowed to explore and do things for himself at the appropriate age; the child who has experienced many kinds of overstimulating experiences such as the excessively seductive parent or the brutal parent; the child with abnormal endocrine development, such as precocious or delayed puberty, and the psychological problems pertaining thereto; and the adoptive child who is curious about his origins.

There is no universal formula for dealing with these many critical psychological events in childhood. What one must remember is that children are not "little adults" but human beings in the process of growth and development. As such, they do not perceive the world and its experiences, and are not equipped to do so, in the same way as adults. Their equipment is incomplete, and therefore their perceptions and feelings about many things are quite different from ours. They are fragile, yet plastic. If we as helping adults can project ourselves into these situations, if we have a genuine appreciation of how a particular situation may appear to a child at a particular stage of development, it is quite likely that we can help to devise ways and means of meeting a particular child's psychological needs. We need to aid and encourage parents to be more honest with their young children. Children may be small, but they have feelings about the complexities of life's events. They need the freedom to talk about their feelings and to ask questions. They need some answers, but we do not have to know all the answers to all the questions they ask. They can accept our not knowing if we are honest, rather than evasive, when we do not know. We can wonder with them about many things.

Simple discussions with a young child about the death of a pet, a friend, or relative; appropriate responses to early questions about sex; explanations about hospitalization and surgical procedures; recognition of a young child's right to be angry with you but not to hurt you; talks about winning and losing and how the game is played—all these and hundreds of other intimacies shared by young children and adults have enormous immunizing value. If these things can be discussed honestly and frankly by adults—and it is not always easy to do so—the child will begin to build a solid view of the realities of life. Then, when he is confronted with some major psychological event there will be substances of experience in his personality makeup to combat the noxious agents that confront him, in much the same manner that a body, already having grappled with the attenuated virus in vaccines, has developed antibodies that enable it to withstand the virulent strains of germs when they come along.

By the time a child needs residential treatment, many events of significance have taken place. Singly or collectively these critical events, whatever they are, may not have been handled very well by the child and the significant adults.

The work of a child-caring staff is complex and difficult, for it must be directed to attempts at repair of past wounds. At the same time the current program of psychological immunization will have to proceed with even more care. Far more critical events will occur, and it is never too late to begin. The plasticity of human response is encouraging, and immunization begun even at a late date can be beneficial.

CHAPTER 7

The Arrogant Child

*Behind the mask of arrogance
stands the child*

THE RUNNING BOY

Last week he raged.
"I'm leaving this damned place.
Go ahead,
Send me up the river.
No one's telling me
What to do.
I'm tired of people messing,
Trying to run my life.
I don't need your help
Or anyone else's."
He slammed out.

Today he sent word
He wouldn't be there.
I sent a note by runner
To his school.
"I know you're mad with me
But I wish you'd come today."

After track practice he came
Slowly with aching feet.
We talked awhile and then

He put his feet up.
"When I fly off the handle
And hit someone, a friend,
For almost nothing,
It scares me later to think
That I might have hurt them
Or even killed them dead.
That's when I feel like
Running from myself."

"Sometimes I wish I could run
Like a deer escaping
From a hunter.
But when I run
I always feel I'm both
The hunter and the hunted.
I wish I could run,
Forgetting,
Through the next few years
And one day wake up
And find no need
To run at all."

In children's homes and treatment centers across the land there are many children and adolescents with high visibility. Their impact on other children and on the staff is often felt as a continuous shock wave. Their attitudes and behaviors often elicit highly negative reactions in a community, which can threaten the very existence of the program. These youngsters are often called arrogant. Therapeutic work with them is difficult, frustrating, time-consuming, sometimes dangerous, and, to say the least, exhausting both physically and emotionally.

If one looks up *arrogant* in a dictionary, one finds many synonyms and related meanings with a considerable degree of shading. Among hundreds of such descriptive words the following are typical: *haughty, overbearing, disdainful, offensive, contemptuous, hardened, uncivil, sneering, bold,* as adjectives; *arrogance* is defined as *self-assurance, cockiness, shamelessness, lip, disrespect, flippancy, petulance, outrage, self-glorification, big talk,* and *bluster; to be arrogant* means *to look down on, to ride roughshod over, to presume, to be a law unto oneself, to blow one's trumpet.*

If we were perfectly candid with ourselves, we could probably identify several words in the list that at some time we might use to describe some aspect of our own attitudes and behavior. They would, of course, be the milder words, and they would apply somewhere in the distant past, for who among us would willingly be identified by certain of the harsher words in that list?

Let us recognize, therefore, that the arrogant child, as we are describing him, comes in all gradations. Perhaps a word of caution is in order: Let us not be deceived by the word *arrogant* when we refer to a child, for a child is much more than whatever we convey by that word. It is a word we use at some particular time to describe the attitudes and behavior of a particular child. But if we become fixated on the word and the impression it conveys, we are in great danger of not seeing the forest for the trees. Many trees are necessary to make a forest, and many attributes are necessary to make a child.

This is a time when we are all speaking out against stereotypes. Let us not make of arrogance a stereotype. On the other hand, perhaps we have made a stereotype out of the current expression, "You're stereotyping that person." The abhorrence of stereotyping can reach such proportions that we fail to look for causation. To diagnose, that is, to know, becomes suspect because often diagnosis is equated with labeling or stereotyping. Whatever the social and emotional problems of children, we often simply try to do something with them, put them here or there, in this group or that, with little rationale, hoping that something magical will happen. Sometimes it does, but most often it does not. Diagnosis, knowing causation in childhood, must be imperfect because of the multiple causes involved and because the child is a growing, changing organism. Yet, it need not be a stereotype; it should be a guide to attempted amelioration or treatment if used intelligently.

We would not make the mistake of regarding "arrogant child" as a diagnosis. Use of the term must be viewed only as roughly descriptive, and we need to try to understand what it means for a particular child.

What function does the arrogance serve?

Let us look at a situation with which we are all familiar, and perhaps we can see some value in at least the milder expressions of arrogance. It is generally agreed that one of the important ways in which we all learn as children is that of identification. The young boy or girl is aware of some quality in another that is admired and appropriates the attitudes and behavior of the admired one. This is a pretense on both a conscious and an unconscious level, a borrowing from another. The little boy swaggers and chastises his teammates; the little girl is officious and haughty in her play. Seen in the adult from whom it is borrowed, such behavior may appear quite natural. In the child it may appear absurd. It may even become offensive to other children and adults if carried to excess. But this intense "trying on" of another's qualities is usually short-lived in children. It is all a part of finding out who one is, "the real me."

Such borrowing is not limited to children. The graduate student, the new employee in a firm, the new member of an organization may sometimes take on the coloration of someone seen as the leader, perhaps someone who is feared. Carried too far, this becomes grating and often borders on arrogance. It looks silly and imbecilic because we recognize it as false. It serves some kind of protective function for an individual at a particular time, but in the long run, if continued, it is generally alienating in that individual's interpersonal relationships. Yet identification is a perfectly good mechanism, a mechanism common to us all at some time. It can be quite a useful mechanism, one that helps a child establish an identity of his own or protects a temporarily anxious adult in a new situation.

The three children described below would qualify as arrogant children. All were residents in a children's home or a residential treatment center.

Kilmer, thirteen years old, already had served a stint in training school and was known to police and to almost every "helping" agency in town. He lied; he shoplifted; he broke into homes and stole guns; he ran away from school; he would not obey his parents; he gave passersby "the bird"; he hurled invectives at everyone.

During a year in a psychiatric residential treatment center, he had intervals of relative calm, but one never knew when a dramatic and catastrophic episode would occur. Thus, before an early morning lecture (8:00 A.M.) by one of the psychologists for a group of medical students, Kilmer had surreptitiously broken a window and entered the lecture room. On a conference table at the front of the room he had lined up three ashtrays and, with remarkable psychomotor agility and still more remarkable sphincter control, had deposited equal amounts of fresh feces in the three receptacles. The psychologist, a serendipitous soul, recovered more quickly than the medical students and changed his lecture to "The Origins and Expressions of Anal Hostility."

On another occasion, at high noon on a hot summer day, Kilmer, along with two other children and accompanied by a child-care worker, was on the main street of the city. In front of the largest department store in town, Kilmer simultaneously spied a large grasshopper on the plate-glass window and a large-bosomed lady with a low-cut dress on the street. In one fell swoop Kilmer scooped the grasshopper from the window and flung it down the front of the lady's dress as she entered the store. She went around and around in the revolving door, clawing frantically at the—one supposes—equally startled grasshopper. Meanwhile, Kilmer disappeared instantly in the crowded street and swaggered back to the center.

One morning he commandeered from the parking lot the new car of an occupational therapist and was apprehended a block away by police. At still another time, he ran away with an older boy. The boys hitchhiked about thirty miles to a large lake, took a motorboat from a dock, and headed out on the lake. They were nearing the distant shore when they crashed into an anchored boat. This was not Kilmer's first runaway, but this time he was returned to a training school for an extended stay.

Following training school, he made a marginal adjustment doing odd jobs and living at home. Later he was charged with being an accomplice in a sizable theft and spent almost a year in prison where he labored as a jackhammer operator on a work gang. On release he obtained a job with a private firm as a tree surgeon.

Several years later he was married and since then has made a fairly satisfactory adjustment as far as can be determined.

These are the highlights of a long and troubled story, but some items in this boy's life experiences should be pointed out.

He was not planned for, and his mother and stepfather neglected him early. His parents operated a small business when he was young, and they allowed him to run loose on the street or chastised him for being in the way. He was described as a hyperactive baby, and this grew more apparent in his early childhood. There was constant stimulation from those who frequented his parents' shop. His school experience was one of total frustration, and his basic academic learning skills were poorly developed. He could scarcely read or write and could spell almost no words. Kilmer was small in stature, always gravitating toward older boys for companionship and achieving some kind of temporary acceptance by taking their dares. The boy had been whipped severely by his father when he was small and even into his early teen years.

Because he was a perpetual nuisance at school and among peers, his schoolmates quickly modified his name as a means of taunting him. His middle name was Amos; this soon became "Anus." He would be greeted with "Kilmer Anus," then "Kill-My-Anus," and then, "Hey, there, Kiss-My-Anus."

Parental rejection and neglect, parental inconsistency in discipline, whippings, overstimulation, superficial relationships at all levels, peer rejection, school rejection, failure at every turn, are not uncommon in the history of a child whose level of arrogance and antisocial behavior reaches the proportions found in Kilmer.

If one looks at the succession of agencies through which this boy passed, it would appear that each failed in its efforts to help him. On a second look, however, this is not necessarily true. During his year in the children's treatment center, though he was removed after the boat incident, some helpful things began to happen. He did form a kind of relationship with several staff members, especially his therapist. What this meant to him at the time was not ascertainable. However, after he had been taken to the training school nearby, he asked if he could return to the center as an outpatient. This was permitted, and he continued with the same therapist. One might say that the motivation for his request was his desire to be outside the training school for a brief period of time. Maybe. But each time he came he wanted to say "hello" to a few of the staff, and this was allowed.

After discharge from the training school, he always managed to drop in at the center every two or three months and bring his therapist up to date on what was happening. Between times he would telephone. During his prison stay he sent messages a few times. Soon after he was out, he visited the therapist for a long talk, displaying with considerable pride his increase in height and the rock-hard biceps he had developed while riding the jackhammer. A little later he stopped by to tell about his job with the tree-pruning crew and, later still, to announce his marriage plans.

During all of these years, it was possible to learn something of this boy's feelings about his parents, his fantasies of "getting even" with them, his feelings of embarrassment over his learning problems, his generalized hostility to the world, his sense of smallness (physically and in terms of self-worth), his loneliness masked by his frantic activity and "to hell with you" smirk.

Something of value to him was offered in each of his prolonged "stays-in-residence," as it were. In the children's residence, which he used as a kind of home base, there was the start of a relationship, one he used voluntarily over several years. This no doubt was his first sustained experience of being accepted by significant adults for whatever he was or might become, in spite of his undesirable attitudes and behaviors. Instead of feeling, thinking, and acting all at the same instant, he began some limited thought about behavior. He began to learn that one's feelings could be talked about without fear of condemnation or belittling. The training school and prison provided some degree of protection from his own impulses, a very important component in his rehabilitation. After these phases were over, he again returned to home base, often to share some experience he valued and sometimes, it seemed, seeking some indication of affirmation of his worth.

Denise, fifteen, had been in many foster homes, and her stay in each ended the same way. Her hostile expressions, sarcastic responses, fights with other children, attempts at running away, and sexual acting-out would reach such proportions that each foster home would throw in the towel and demand the girl's immediate removal.

When she left her last foster home, more than a dozen applications to children's homes were refused before one children's home finally agreed to accept this girl. Her name was soon a household word on campus.

None of the children liked her; she was disobedient when houseparents tried to intervene; there were numerous fights; on one occasion she chased a houseparent from the cottage with a switchblade; another time she threw a bottle across a room, striking a girl in the head, the laceration requiring several stitches. Children and staff were afraid of her, and with ample justification. There was much talk among staff that she probably could not be kept in the home, and it appeared that history was on the verge of repeating itself. At this point, she was scheduled to see the consultant.

With some apprehension the consultant arranged to first meet her in the caseworker's office before asking her to come to his office. Knowing that some kind of intervention must take place in this student-staff crisis, the consultant decided to take a risk. Following are some highlights of that first meeting.

"I don't know much about you—nothing about your life before you came here, except what your caseworker and your housemother have told me recently. I understand from them that you've been in many foster homes and none has worked out. They have told me something about that. And, of course, they have told me about the troubles you're having here."

Denise interrupted. "I don't like it here. Everybody's crazy. They don't like me, and I don't want to be here."

"I understand that you don't like it here, and you may have good reasons. But I have to tell you that everybody here isn't crazy. You may not like the people here, but that doesn't make them crazy."

She glared at the consultant, who continued: "This brings me to why you and I are getting together today. Staff tells me you've been kicked out of a lot of places, and the same things are happening here, and they don't want to have to kick you out."

"They don't care."

"It may seem that way, but they do care or you wouldn't be sitting here talking with me. And I think you care but are afraid to admit to yourself or anyone else that you care. From what I am told has happened in the homes you've been in and out of, and now here, you go out of your way to prove to yourself that others don't care."

"What do you mean?" she asked, half interested and half defiant.

"I mean that if you behave in a way that gets everyone angry with you, and if they can no longer put up with your fights and insults, and if they kick you out, then you can once more say to yourself, 'See, they don't really care about me, and I was right all along.'"

She was silent and, with a decided softening of her voice, said, "I don't know how to make friends."

Still quieter, "Yes." Then, with a faint smile, "I sure know just what to do to make someone mad, but I don't know how to make friends."

"If you feel that way, I guess we can help you learn how."

The interview proceeded from there, with Denise revealing much about her past life, her activities and attitudes. Her mother was fifteen when Denise was born, and Denise was expected to look after younger children when only a child herself. When she was an early teenager, her mother in wild rage had stabbed her in the chest with a knife, resulting in considerable loss of blood. This required hospitalization, and she was not returned home after this episode.

Denise kept her weekly appointments with the consultant and continued to take inventory in an attempt to change her destructive patterns of living. Relationships with houseparents and peers changed for the better, and there were no more bottle or switchblade incidents. She said on several occasions that she was glad she had come to the children's home, as it had given her a chance to think about her life. Denise was able to visit her sisters who were in a foster home, and she visited her father a few times. She began to talk about the future in a constructive way and no longer talked about how "ugly" she was.

Denise has much more to do, but through timely intervention and continued work the constant barrage of arrogant expressions and frightening behavior has diminished markedly. Denise has taken a look at herself and likes some at least of what she sees.

Harry was eleven and had been in the children's home for nearly nine months. He treated peers with contempt, and he met adult attempts to guide his activities with defiance, stony silence, or passive-aggressive maneuvers such as agreeing with suggestions but never following through. Attempts at individual counseling had been unproductive. He simply would not talk about his feelings, past experiences, future hopes, or current interpersonal relationships with his peers, except to criticize them.

The boy had been admitted to this particular children's home some time after his father and mother had separated. His behavior at home, with the mother and three younger sisters, had been such that outpatient attempts at counseling had been to no avail. Actually, he was admitted to the children's home from a detention home where he had been taken after he had literally demolished a classroom at school.

The director of the children's home said one day in some despair, "Harry has been here almost a year and has not changed at all. If we can't do something soon to alter his alienating ways he's going to have a poor prospect of changing. Besides, he's almost ready to move into puberty, and in his present condition he'll be a holy terror."

Thus began for Harry and a consultant psychiatrist an episodic year characterized by a very difficult beginning. He acted silly much of the time and responded to even the most casual inquiry about his feelings surrounding some current event with either silence or a short, hostile remark. Initially, he and the consultant spent much of the time playing card games, at Harry's instigation. He found it very hard to lose, becoming angry or defiant and sometimes accusing the therapist of cheating. He was quite good at several games and took great delight in remarking acidly on the stupidity of his opponent.

Focusing on the therapist's stupidity became his style for a long time and generalized from cards to almost everything. At some point after a sustained diatribe the therapist would comment that Harry certainly was angry and that, in the therapist's opinion, he had not really done anything to merit such disapproval. Or the therapist might say that Harry reminded him of a boy he once knew who did the same thing to the therapist but who was angry about many other things.

One day Harry said unexpectedly that he liked coming to therapy each week because he could tell the therapist everything he didn't like about him to his face and he did not get angry.

From this time he gradually began to talk about his feelings. He remembered his parents arguing at night and was afraid they would kill each other. He remembered threats of their leaving and worried about what would happen to him and his sisters. Then one night his mother told his father to leave and never come back. Slowly, from week to week, Harry disclosed a little more. He knew his parents had problems, but he kept hoping for their reunion. After his father left, he resented his mother's men friends. He began to act out against his mother, showing defiance, stealing, lying, or acting contemptuously toward her. School work went rapidly downhill. On the day that he tore the classroom apart, a teacher had reprimanded him for some smart-aleck remark. His mother said she couldn't control him, and he was taken to a detention home and then to the children's home. He said, "They've put me away, in prison, but all the problems ain't mine."

The mother remarried and moved to another state. The father became involved in a counseling relationship. Harry's attitudes and behavior improved. He began to talk about wanting to leave the children's home, but he was in anguish about where he should go. After agonizing over his loyalties to each of the parents, he finally elected to live with his father and visit with his mother and sisters from time to time.

The father, sometime before Harry's departure from the children's home, had been offered a job in another country that he could ill afford to turn down. The therapist's and Harry's last session together on the day he was to catch a plane to join his father was a memorable one. Harry was aware of his anxiety about living with his father in another country, where he would attend a bilingual school and know no one. The boy had talked for many hours about his situation and what it would be like in a strange country. He had admired a Big Red Parker pen used by the therapist, so as a surprise going-away present the therapist gave him an identical fountain pen with the admonition to teach it to write Spanish.

On the last day, a very rainy one, he spent a good part of the time wearing the therapist's raincoat, which dragged on the floor, and hat, with the Big Red pen in his shirt pocket. He went up and down the hall, dropping into offices and chatting briefly with staff. This was a kind of dress rehearsal for the unknown ahead, and in his own way he was taking a part of his therapist with him.

A year later Harry stopped by the children's home, en route to visit with his mother. It had been a good year. He and his father had had their minor ups and downs, and he had had a good visit with his mother and sisters at Christmas. He had done well in school. He could speak Spanish, and Big Red had learned to write Spanish. He had grown considerably, and as he left he laughed and told the therapist, "I bet your raincoat wouldn't drag the floor if I wore it now."

These are just three cases, in each of which one gets a brief inner view of a child's feelings. All three youngsters had experienced in their young lives a climate of toxicity and a series of catastrophic events that resulted in gross interference with normal personality development.

Kilmer was the most lacking in trust, a quality that needs to begin developing in the first year of life, for it is on a sense of early trust in others that further development must depend.

Denise, who must have had some of this trust in infancy and early childhood, was deficient in the area of autonomy. That is, she had been given heavy responsibility early without any consistent, flexible guidance. She was criticized and treated harshly when she erred. This was conducive to a low sense of self-esteem and self-worth. If she tried to do something right, in the view of her mother she was usually wrong, and if she didn't try at all she was wrong. There was no safe emotional space in which she could move.

Harry was frightened and devastated when his fairly secure world began to crumble and then became an avalanche; his developing initiative was nipped in the bud. His subsequent frantic, irrational outbursts came as he was in an almost continual state of panic.

These were three quite different children, but all three deserved enough of the descriptive terms we have assembled to be called "arrogant" by even a passerby. All three were overbearing, contemptuous, disdainful, disrespectful, flippant, blustering, pretending, offensive. For each the arrogance served as a kind of armor. One can visualize an inscription on this armor of arrogance that might read: "I've been hurt, I'm vulnerable, and I don't want to be hurt any more. A good offense is the best defense."

The problem was that the offense engaged in by these children to defend themselves was offensive to those around. It provided an immediate, short-lived protection, but in the long run it was destructive to these children in that it alienated them from others; and in the long run we need these others, if we are to live with any degree of satisfaction.

Each of these children was well on the road to making the mode of arrogance a way of life. Each might have somehow worked things out in his own manner. But as such reactions become more fixed, more rigid, as a part of a child's personality, they become less amenable to change. There is some reason to believe that the intervention that took place helped to move these children out of the self-destructive ruts in which they were stuck and back on a more productive, satisfying road.

If we reflect on even the limited material presented, it is apparent that a decided change took place in each child. That change occurred through the slow process of another person's becoming a part of the child's life to the extent that the other person no longer presented a major threat to the child's inner life. Thus, each child could in his or her own way begin to tolerate the feelings he or she was asked to examine. Some of these feelings were discarded and others put into better perspective.

There are many things going on at any one time in such a

process. There is involvement, which means, "I have time for you. It is consistent, predictable time, so let's get together and come to know each other. It may help." There is a relationship that grows. It may at times be very positive. It may at times be negatively charged. There is catharsis or ventilation, a time for "unloading," and often in the unloading the child begins to hear what he is saying. Some of what he is saying may after a time sound pretty unrealistic. Everybody may not be all bad. What provoked the child to attack someone verbally or otherwise may have been completely unintended by the other person. So there is the beginning of insight and improved reality testing.

In Harry's case there was evidence of considerable sublimation in the competitive card games that were played. Later there was identification as he became the teacher and helped the therapist improve his skills. A different quality of identification was reflected in his wearing the raincoat.

All of these processes add up to the probability that the child has increased his sense of self-worth and self-esteem and thus will have greater flexibility in interpersonal relationships and consequently a greater repertory of coping skills. If this is the case, arrogance will no longer be necessary. The child can get past that and on with other matters.

A fifteen-year-old boy who had been resident in a children's home for nearly two years and who was about ready to return home once made some poignant observations. This adopted boy had, a few years earlier, become "unmanageable" at home after his father died. The mother was disturbed and disturbing. The boy had gone the drug route, from pot to glue to LSD; he was stealing, lying, and running away. His surface behavior was arrogant by any standard, but beneath this "protective" behavior was a severely depressed youth who was quite disorganized and whose reality testing was severely impaired at times.

Before leaving the children's home he wanted to sum up what the experience had meant to him. "I'm glad I came," he said, "but I didn't think that way for several months. I thought everybody was against me, trying to prove that I was crazy. The truth is I had been afraid myself for a long time that I was crazy. I've really done some crazy things."

Of his therapist he said, "He was there week after week. He didn't say much, but I could tell that he kind of knew how I was feeling. When I was lying, or acting cool, or saying some pretty 'kooky' things, he didn't tell me I was doing that. He may have asked a question now and then that made me think about something. Most of all, he didn't change—I mean he didn't clobber me or criticize me or make me feel I was no good, though often that's how I felt. He always saw through all that and made me feel like somebody, someone for real, mainly by his attitude. I know what it was—he was more like an anchor, always there to quiet things down when the boat was rocking. Sometimes the storm was of my own making, sometimes someone else's, but usually a combination. Even if I went into that room in a rage, I always felt better when I left. After a long time I began to look at life in a different way, and now I think I can see all right."

This boy appears to have captured the essence of some important elements in the treatment process. Each child is different. Each comes from life experiences that differ in quantity and quality. For those who try to be of help, it is important to be able to see these children as being of value, as being worthwhile. Different children will require different approaches to treatment, and nearly all will require patience and forgiveness, for there will be inevitable failures and disappointments. In trying to design a treatment plan for a particular child, we shall need to look not only at the child and what he brings with him but at ourselves as well. For our attitudes are of paramount importance in the rearing of our children, and especially important in the attempt at treatment of the child we have described as arrogant.

Arrogance is not limited to childhood, and the arrogant adult is grossly limited in any attempt at helping the arrogant child.

CHAPTER 8

Communicating with the Adolescent

Anxieties, doubts, joys, and expectations

SQUELCH

With one fell swoop of tongue
Young Lady
You put me in proper place
One day
You jauntily tossed
Your head and said
"There's only one fault
With you, Dad
You don't understand
Anything
About children.
Go away."

In our society the adolescent is neither a child nor an adult; this prolonged period of development has its own peculiar characteristics. It is a time of special vulnerability, and during this time many adolescents in passage become lost at sea or run aground in treacherous waters. Adolescents with emotional problems severe enough to require care and treatment in residential group settings pose a special challenge. It would be encouraging if we as parents could learn to guide our children through the earlier years in such a way as to eliminate the need for these specialized programs; but so far this is not the case.

Many unusual problems arise in attempting to develop an effective treatment program for emotionally disturbed adolescents, and some of them have already been mentioned. Perhaps one of the major difficulties is the individual and collective staff attitudes toward adolescents, which vary greatly from person to person and from program to program. The successful treatment of adolescents is never easy, but it is often less effective and more debilitating to staff because we lose sight of what adolescence is all about. Those who work with adolescents must keep foremost in mind where adolescents are going, how they get there, and what tasks they must complete.

Almost everyone who lives or works with an adolescent recognizes that there is a communication problem. To many adults adolescents are strange, unreasonable creatures who live in a world of their own, unheeding of all advice and deaf to all pleading. Part of the problem may, however, lie in our adult selves. We may have forgotten what it is like to be an adolescent, or we may remember only those things about our own adolescence that we wish to remember.

There is a progression of human personality growth and development from cradle to grave. A person moves from one stage to the next, with many stages overlapping. Some of the tasks that must be accomplished are easy to manage, and others are difficult. All along the continuum one deals with the developmental sequences with varying degrees of success. Most of us are left with solid strengths in certain areas and relative weaknesses and vulnerabilities in others.

Adolescence covers a long period of time, with many hurdles to surmount. It is a time when many tasks begun in early life have to be brought to a fairly high degree of resolution if one is to move into adulthood with a good chance of successfully assuming the privileges and responsibilities of a grownup.

It is a difficult period, filled with anxieties and doubts as well as joys and expectations. If one chooses to dwell on its problems alone, one wonders how anyone ever traverses this ill-defined belt between childhood and adulthood. Yet, however difficult and filled with pitfalls this time may be, most of us seem to make it through and emerge as fairly intact adults with the capacity for working, for finding someone to love, and for becoming parents ourselves.

If we make it, and have not landed in jail or in a mental institution, we may, in fact, consider ourselves well versed in the tricky art of growing up. But upon becoming young adults we move into another phase of life that is all-consuming of time, thought, and action as we try to find our way in a competitive world. We are grateful to be there, but the pace is such that there is not much time or inclination to think about the adolescence behind us. We got through it somehow, and it soon begins to look, through the distance of years, like an impressionistic painting: we recognize that it is there and what it is, but the details are not very clear. Certain events we remember, although they are subject to the distortion of the lens of time—things like a winning touchdown, a long-awaited date with a particular girl, our first payday when we worked at the corner market—things that made us feel good, enhanced our self-esteem, and one by one added to our storehouses and helped us to feel good about being ourselves.

At the same time many things about adolescence we do not remember, or we remember them imperfectly. Some things flit like ghosts in the darkened recesses on the stage of the conscious mind, often right in the middle of some activity we are enjoying. We try to banish these intruders back into the wings as quickly as possible. In our own adolescence, there were many ideas and experiences that made us feel uneasy, unworthy, afraid, anxious, or guilty. Naturally we repressed totally or partially those incidents that were most threatening and that made us most uncomfortable. This psychological reflex of repression, and many other psychological mechanisms of defense, are as automatic as a child's withdrawal of his finger from a hot stove. They serve a similar purpose—to protect us in one case from further physical harm and in the other from a level of anxiety that can be extremely uncomfortable and even disorganizing of function.

Yet, there is no way to get from here to there, from childhood to adulthood, without going through adolescence, without experiencing both its joys and its anxieties. This is how character develops and how individuals are made. It may well be that lurking anxieties from our own adolescence need no longer be so threatening, if we only knew it. They are there to an extent in all of us, and one suspects that the spasmodic, jerky, erratic, shifting, arrogant, sure yet unsure behavior of adolescent youth touches the hidden hurts within each of us from the past. We do not like to be reminded of these hurts; they are too painful. Rather than run the risk, we have to protect ourselves by building a wall between ourselves and the current crop of youth. We disapprove of everything about them. Whereas our own adolescence looks like an impressionistic painting to us, the current behavior of youth sometimes reminds us of a surrealistic nightmare.

They say that we do not understand, and they are partly right. But perhaps we understand more than we are given credit for. Further, if we could realize that our own adolescent ghosts need not be so alarming today, we might be of greater help in providing guidance to the current generation.

Once the growth spurt starts, with its accompanying changes, physical and emotional, the young adolescent is rapidly catapulted into a dilemma about parents. From infancy, when the child was totally helpless and had to depend on nurturing figures for everything, he developed a view of parents as being all-knowing and all-powerful. Parents were needed, and they responded. This early view of parents has already changed somewhat as the child moves from being a lap baby to a knee baby to a yard baby and out into the neighborhood. The child gradually gains some independence and some sense of being an individual. As the child moves into early adolescence, the whole self undergoes a sudden change—new thoughts, new emotions, new ways of perceiving himself and his world—as he strives to find an identity as an autonomous individual. The young adolescent is still more child than adult, and the earlier view of parents is still part of him. But even with the optimal relationship with parents as a solid background, the adolescent will writhe, moan, and protest the parents' decisions, whatever they are, as they threaten his autonomy. If the parents have been actually neglectful, rejecting, or even cruel, this may be a really stormy time. The youth often wants parents with a different set of values and approaches, and much of the protest, both verbal and behavioral, may communicate this, but the adolescent may have to come to the realization that little can be done directly to change parents. The past one cannot change, but it is possible to change one's own attitudes and behavior.

The real danger at this time is that parents do not recognize the adolescent's struggle and view every negative statement and attitude as hateful and insubordinate. Often the youth's anger, irrational though it may be, is met with equally irrational adult anger that drives the two generations further apart. This freeing of himself from dependence on his parents is the goal of the adolescent's conflicting emotions, but if it is accomplished with continuing bilateral hostility and rejection, it leaves lingering scars. During this time something needs to remain fairly stable, and it must be the parents because the adolescent is not stable and cannot be so until he gradually finds an identity as an individual moving toward adulthood. The adolescent's vacillation should be our cue, and if we recognize that this is a time-limited proposition, friction will be lessened. Many parents do not recognize this and make matters worse. Guidance from a counselor in getting this point across to parents is just as important as helping an adolescent to understand that parents are not all good or all bad, that in fact they are like other people. Eventually the adolescent comes to this view of parents, but only after considerable time and much practice.

The adolescent is also moving toward the ultimate selection of a marriage partner, but before this can be successful his own sexual identity must be consolidated. This might seem to be an easy task as sex is genetically determined, but a great deal of practice is necessary in learning to be a boy or a girl. This learning starts quite early as the child observes father and mother and their behavior. Here is the point at which many distorted views of man and woman begin. There is the punitive or cruel parent of either sex; there is the seductive parent who has such an unsatisfactory relationship with the marriage partner that he or she leans on a young child for emotional gratification; and there is the home in which one parent is missing and there is no suitable substitute to serve as a sex model for the child.

Even if the young child comes through the family triangle period satisfactorily, these relationships are activated again with the onset of puberty and early adolescence. Part of the protest about parental relationships has to do with sexual feelings. Parents often contribute to intensifying this difficult period by extreme attitudes of affection and rejection. Especially in broken homes is this a problem, and it is surprising how often a mother has a pubescent boy sleeping in her room or even in her bed, or a father has a highly seductive relationship with a pubescent daughter. These are unwholesome relationships that are potentially crippling to the young adolescent.

On a milder scale, most young adolescents are concerned with a multitude of questions and doubts about their emerging sexuality. Will I be male enough, or female enough? What about penis size, or breast size? Much information is obtained from peers, but much of it is distorted. Some information is available from parents, but there are many questions children feel that they cannot ask their parents. Such information is best obtained from a neutral source, from a teacher, a counselor, or a physician.

A young adolescent becomes concerned about dating, the strength of sexual feelings, masturbation, petting, intercourse, and marriage and needs someone to listen to his thoughts and questions. Such a relationship probably develops best out of a continuing preadolescent relationship with some person such as a doctor or a youth leader, a relationship in which the adolescent does not fear that every concern will be revealed to curious parents watching and listening in the outer office. However immature and arcane his thoughts and acts may sometimes be, the adolescent is searching for identity and deserves some dignity in this search, deserves to be taken seriously. It is reassuring and healing to adolescents to find that most fears are universal and that they do, indeed, still belong to the human race. This kind of validation for a troubled youngster is of inestimable value. One day the adolescent may smile or actually laugh at himself, a pretty good sign of maturation.

Conscience formation begins early in the child's life and at first is largely a reflection of the sanctions and disapprovals of the father and mother. Parents have their own codes of conduct and behavior, but the family is also the primary source for transmitting the taboos and sanctions of the culture. At first these are external matters, but the child gradually begins to comply in response to signals of approval or disapproval. Soon those "dos and don'ts" are made a part of the developing personality, and the child begins to exercise some internal controls. As growth continues, the formation of conscience or ethical concepts is aided by other sources—school, church, Scouts, and various communication media.

The process continues throughout the adolescent years. In fact a "shaking up" occurs here because the youth is in touch with a much wider circle of friends, often from different backgrounds and different parts of the country. Peers at this age are the people with whom the adolescent must succeed, and it is inevitable that there will be some "loosening" as well as some "tightening" of the conscience during these years. The adolescent must emerge with a fairly solid code of conduct, and as parents watch the evidences of conflict over right and wrong in their children they are frequently alarmed that what they have tried to instill will be washed away by the incessant waves of change. The chances are, however, that although change will occur the adolescent will emerge from these struggles with an ethic not markedly different from what the family taught in the formative years. This is a time when young people need to try out ideas not only with peers but with a more neutral observer than the immediate family.

The problem of choosing one's life's work can cause great consternation; young people are under pressure to commit themselves earlier and earlier. Adolescents tend to see everything as in the present, and time seems foreshortened. It is unfortunate to have to make such a decision so early; yet the pressure is there, at least to move in some general direction. Perhaps we might do better than we have in helping adolescents to decide whether college or vocational training, or still another possibility should be the next goal. Perhaps we might help some of them feel more comfortable with the choice that circumstances direct them to take. Perhaps those of us who know something about feelings and perceptions are in position to help adolescents feel better about themselves and their choices.

Of prime importance is the capacity of the counselor to empathize with the adolescent. To do so one needs to be enough in touch with one's own adolescent years to remember some of the pains as well as the pleasures. It helps to know many adolescents, not just as patients or pupils but under other circumstances, such as in church groups, athletic teams, Scouts, or boys' or girls' clubs. A good way of getting the flavor of adolescents' "inner life" is through reading fiction about them. Writers often are able to express meaningful insights into thinking and feeling.

A counselor should maintain a friendly objectivity. One has to be oneself; adolescents do not want an adult to try to be adolescent with them. That only adds to their confusion. They do want to feel that someone is trying to understand how they feel. That in itself lessens the sense of isolation. The adult should also be alert to transference, realizing that adolescents will have a strong tendency to react to a counselor as they do to their parents, especially if the parents sent them for counseling. Their relationship to the counselor may then be filled with hostility, behind which is fear. If anger elicits counteranger, hostility, and rejection from the counselor, the youngsters are not helped. It is only further proof that all adults are alike and do not understand. The adult has to make it clear that anger does no harm and that he or she is not the parent. The counselor may need to form an alliance with the adolescents to assure them the details of what is said will not be revealed to the parents. The youngsters may need to know that if there is some major problem the parents will have to know, but they need reassurance that less crucial matters important to a young person will be held in confidence.

The counselor also has a responsibility to try to help wellmeaning parents to understand the meaning of the struggles an adolescent is going through, yet support them in major decisions. Sometimes adolescents must be protected from their own impulses, but the counselor can help to keep parents from interfering every time their children move.

In dealing with young people, one should not be too quick to put a name or a label on an emotional state, as this may frighten an adolescent. Adolescents typically have all the symptoms of psychiatric disorders; yet many of these symptoms are transient and normal at that age. For instance, all adolescents show at times symptoms of depression. The adolescent is losing his or her childhood and dependency and at the same time struggling and fighting for independence. It is enough to depress anyone. They somehow know they cannot have their cake and eat it too, but that does not mean they like it that way.

An adult must be honest with an adolescent; if he does not know an answer he should say so but express the wish to help find a satisfactory solution. This attitude indicates respect to which a young person will respond. A counselor should spend more time listening than talking. "Nobody listens to me" is often an adolescent's chief complaint. If one listens with a nod or sound of encouragement, youngsters will be likely to find their own solutions to perplexing problems. Then the young person has done the work and can take pride in the accomplishment.

Throughout all of the struggles of these young people, it is well to keep in mind that they are trying to find an identity—What am I? Who am I? Where am I going? And how will I get there? Their means of doing this are often ineffectual, time-consuming, and wasteful. The counselor's task is to help them chart a course and start them on their long journey as safely as possible.

CHAPTER 9

Play and Recreation

Play serves many functions

MICK

Mick felt good today
made me feel the same
wanted to sing and play
said he'd practiced a lot.

Showing improving skills
he played the piano hot
throwing in some frills
experimenting all the way.

Two janitors came and stood
pleased with what they heard
picking up the groovy mood
that Mick sang and played.

Then he slowed it down
smiled with twinkling glee
"You know what I've found?
It ain't all bad being me."

Christmas was approaching, and the spirits of the children soared as preparations got underway for the annual Christmas pageant. The pageant was eagerly anticipated by children and staff alike, for it was a combined effort on the part of everyone in this residential treatment center.

John, a small nine-year-old boy, had come to the center in September of that year after authorities in the district became concerned that he was not attending school. He had gone to school the first day or two, reluctantly, but had refused to attend after that. Efforts had been made to help the parents seek assistance from one of the community agencies, but they had not done so. Both parents had found work after their recent move to the community, after having moved many times in the past few years. They admitted that they were concerned about John but said they could not take time from their jobs to deal with his problems. John stayed at home by day where a neighbor checked on him occasionally, but he continued to refuse to attend school.

As the weeks went on, pressure was brought on the parents to "do something about the boy," and they finally agreed to a diagnostic evaluation at a children's treatment center a hundred miles away. The clinic staff thought that the boy could benefit from short-term residential treatment, and the parents agreed to come to the center to visit every other weekend.

One of John's problems had been his inability to read. It was not clear at first whether he had reading skills or whether for reasons of his own he simply would not make any effort. At any rate, during the short time that he had been in residence, working with a teacher in a one-to-one relationship, he had begun to read in a very unskilled way. As the relationship with the teacher grew, he timidly confided to her that he had been ashamed to try to read in public school because he did not know how and others laughed at him. During the fall, the boy's reading skills improved by leaps and bounds, and his socialization improved markedly.

When the time came for casting the parts in the Christmas pageant, the teacher decided to ask John whether he would be interested in the narrator's job. He was hesitant at first but obviously pleased that he had been asked; and he agreed to try with the teacher's help. Much work went into preparation for this task—much practice both individually with the teacher and before the group of which he had become a part.

The day of the pageant finally arrived. Many parents and other invited guests were present, including John's parents, who were greatly pleased at the total progress their son was making.

The pageant went off without any major hitches, and it was indeed a fine production. Several visitors in the audience knew of John's inability to read when he had entered the program and were aware how much he had progressed. As soon as the pageant was over, one visitor went up to John and said, "That was a fine job you did, young man. You are a fine reader."

John beamed, and he pulled himself to his fullest height, looked directly at the woman, and said, "Yes, ma'am. I'm the best goddamn reader in this place."

"You certainly are," said the woman, smiling and giving him an affectionate pat on the back.

Was this play? Was it recreation? Was it work? Was it school? Was it therapy? We believe that it was all of these, a combination of many things that had great meaning for this particular boy.

Recreation should be viewed broadly, because it combines many elements that can make a great contribution to growing self-esteem and a positive self-image. Play is sometimes described as a pleasurable, self-directed process, with no product involved. That may frequently be the case, but if one takes a careful look there are many tangible and intangible products or outcomes involved in play, whether the play is planned or unplanned. Play is important and can contribute positively to a child's growth.

At one time play may be strictly a relationship between a child and an adult. Over a period of time the child develops a sense of trust in that relationship. There are many children who do not know how to play, and only through this relationship can the freedom come to trust oneself and to involve oneself in play. Involvement grows out of the relationship, and it may take many forms. For a period of time it may be solitary play in the presence of another or it may be parallel play with another person, and eventually it may be shared play with another adult or child. When it reaches the point of shared play, a great deal of change has taken place in the child's capacity to trust and degree of socialization.

At another time play may be a process of ventilation of pent-up frustrations, anger, and tensions; and the person involved in the setting with the child may be the object of this ventilation. How such expressions are handled is extremely important. They need to be handled in such a way that the child is not "forced inside himself" again. The very fact that the child feels that he can express his frustrations without fear of retaliation says something important about the child's perception of the relationship. As the relationship grows, the child develops more self-esteem, and as frustrations are ventilated and tensions lowered, the need for this kind of cathartic ventilation will decrease.

Sometimes play may be sublimation, and the child may, with the aid of an adult, channel aggressions and hostile impulses into the play in a direct manner. This can take the form of banging or beating on pounding boards or whatever is at hand; or it can take the form of smearing with finger paints. It can take the form of wish fulfillment through artistic productions in clay or paints. It can take the form of participation in organized bodily contact sports, such as football, and this can channel hostile-aggressive impulses into an acceptable outlet. If so, it is at the same time providing the child with the structure in which the rules of the game are set forth and through which there is interaction with many other children, thus contributing to socialization.

For another child, play may be identification with another person—an admired older child, an adult, a parent, a teacher, or a celebrity whose qualities the child admires. The identification may take many forms, such as adopting the same batting stance as an admired baseball player or the same posture and gait as an admired older person. In any event it is a "trying on" of some characteristic or quality which at the moment the child wants as a part of himself.

At different times, for some children, play becomes reality testing. It tests what is acceptable and what is not and what the consequences are. Sometimes play becomes an overcompensation for something children know or sense is missing from their lives. This kind of play may be "inside," "outside," or both. By *inside* one means the fantasy life of the child, and by *outside* the expressive life of the child. The fantasy or play behavior can become so engrossing as to enable the child to escape, at least temporarily, from the oppressions in fact or fantasy in real life. Play may be all of these things for a child at one time or another.

With understanding and guidance on the part of the recreation specialist and other staff members in a residential setting, all of these processes can lead the child to some degree of understanding and insight into his own personality. As a result, the child's coping abilities will increase in strength, thereby improving his chances of leading a more gratifying life and at the same time contributing to the social group of which, to some extent, he must always be a part, wherever he may find himself.

Play, then, is living and learning, and at the same time it can be psychotherapeutic. Most assuredly, we believe that play should be gratifying, but at the same time we must recognize that there are times of frustration as well. In the long run, a product is always involved, though it may not have measurable dimensions and a clear-cut definition. The product in play or recreation may be an idea, an object, or an event.

One aspect of play and recreation that is gratifying in and of itself is that it is a continuing process. One does not pass or fail once and for all; and there is always another time and place to try, with the additional benefit of the understanding and insight that one has gained from previous experience. Play can help in some degree to master one's thoughts, impulses, skills, and relationships.

A recreation program is not an activity that can be totally developed outside of and around the child. For recreation to succeed in behalf of the child, which is its aim, the child's characteristics and level of development must always be the foremost consideration. For instance, everyone who works with young children is aware of the stages through which they move in their play. The young infant explores its own body with its hands and its immediate surroundings with its eyes. Gradually the mother or the primary child-caring agent is included, and the child busily explores with its near receptors this immediate microcosmic world. The child looks at and "takes in" its mother's face with its eyes. It feels the configuration of her face with its hands, as it earlier explored the breasts during the nursing procedure; it tastes with its taste buds and is pleased or displeased; it explores the immediate environment with its olfactory sense; and it is ever alert to sounds, both familiar and strange, in its immediate surroundings. These activities may not be viewed as strictly play, but there is often an element of play present. This kind of play is basically preparation for survival, and a great amount of learning is going on at any time in the course of these explorations by the newborn.

One sees a gradual unfolding of some of these elements into activities that are usually thought of as more directly associated with play. An example is the "hide-and-seek" activity in which an infant engages with its mother or other known adults. When the mother's face reappears, one can see the expression of pleasure on the infant's face. As the child becomes a little older, the element of play continues in many activities. At one time the baby becomes interested in throwing or dropping an object and expresses pleasure as the mother or someone else starts to retrieve the object. Or the infant experiences frustration and babbles its protest when the object is not returned.

As the child gains mobility, there is an ever-recurring hiding and reappearing from the mother or the child-caring person. This may not be called play, but it certainly has an element of play about it, and a great deal of learning is connected with it. What happens when I go away? Does she come after me? Will she be there when I get back? One can formulate many questions about the small world of the child and the child's activities in exploring and discovering what that world is like. It is play; it is recreation; it is learning; it is socialization.

All of these activities are connected with learning about the world and the child's place in it, and the kinds of play and the areas of play are continually expanding. When the child is in the preschool years, one sees much play connected with the family constellation itself, and as the child gets a little older, this expands to include significant figures in the community—the pediatrician, the storekeeper, the neighbor next door, and many others. Watching small children play with figures representing family members gives a definite impression that this, too, is a part of the child's way of familiarizing itself not only with self but with the other people who make up society for the child. The parental figures in this kind of family play carry out the functions of adults, and sometimes one sees the child taking on these functions in relation to other doll figures. This kind of play becomes very much a part of children's relationships with each other in that one child "becomes" the mother, another the father; and one hears language spoken that is often an exact replica of what the child hears and what the child perceives as parental attitudes and roles. At least part of what is taking place here is identification with adults, with the authority they represent and the power they exercise. The child tries to appropriate some of this and through this appropriation comes a little closer to understanding its relationship to the towering figures around.

It is easy to see how this early play, recreation, and learning serve many functions for the child. What are these things, people, objects, events, sounds, odors, activities around me? What do they do? Why do they do it? Can I do the same thing? What can I do? How can I interact with the many stimuli around me? What is the result of my interaction? What impact do I have on another child? What can a ball do? What can it do by itself? What can it do when I throw it? Who will bring it back? Can I go where the ball has landed and bring it back myself? Why is the ball round? What is round? Why does a ball roll? Why will a block not roll? Millions of questions are ever present, if one stops to think about it. Each endeavor on the part of the child is an attempt at exploring, understanding, and learning about itself and its world. Uninhibited, there is a natural inner thrust to play.

As the child moves into the late preschool and early school years, more structure is introduced. There are many other children out there, who are at the same time busy doing the same things that this child is doing. Now, as a part of their socialization, children are exposed to a cultural blueprint of what behavior is acceptable and what not acceptable. The idea of structure begins to emerge and have a greater impact. Rules of the game are superimposed, and soon the children are developing their own games with their own kinds of rules. At first these rules may be very simple and, from an adult's viewpoint, illogical. They may be subject to modification and change as the situation changes. The child is still centered in its own world and may want to change a rule unilaterally so as to better gratify its needs at that particular moment.

At a later date, such behavior becomes unacceptable to other children and to supervising adults; and the child is up against a more rigid structure. Alone, in the face of the group, the child is unable to modify the rules to gratify an immediate wish. There are therefore two main avenues open. In great frustration, the child may become a nonparticipant; or, as eventually happens for most of us, the child may accept the rules of the game for what they are and find freedom of movement in being, for the time, in that particular game. If rules are then to be changed, it becomes the function of negotiation and consensus. Rules and conformity have become a part of the group's experience, and the child's degree of socialization expands further through this process.

This spiral of growth and development, including socialization, continues, and as age increases and experience widens the child in play and recreation comes closer to seeing himself as a part of society and at the same time as an individual with unique qualities. In other words, through this process a unique identity is gradually gained. The child is more aware of alikeness and differentness in relation to others; he also comes to some awareness that being an individual and at the same time being a part of the group are not mutually exclusive but complementary to each other.

The child learns many roles and is thus able to put himself "in the place of the other." This flexibility is certainly a mark of civilization and is an indication that the child has moved away from the egocentric mode so prevalent in the early process of socialization. It is a bigger world, but the whole world does not revolve around the child; and through these interactions in play and recreation, the child is better able to know himself and others.

Thus far we have spoken mainly about the matter of play and recreation in relationship to others, and this is a vital consideration. At the same time, one should not overlook the importance of play and recreation as a solitary pursuit for the individual. It may well be that in a pluralistic society with a plethora of values we sometimes tend to overemphasize group participation as the all-important aspect of socialization. Ultimately, group participation is extremely important, but at the same time we must not overlook the individual's need for self-expression through recreation and play. For many reasons that are not altogether clear, we do appear to differ in the degree of intensity and in the ways in which we involve ourselves in groups.

Untimely and too intense pressure for group play and group

participation may, in some instances, only isolate a child further. Therefore, it is important to achieve some kind of balance so that the child has not only the group participation but the support and encouragement of significant adults to pursue particular interests that may not involve others. In and of itself, a solitary pursuit does not necessarily mean isolation from the group. It may mean that a child can better develop a capacity for creative and renewing activity as an individual; and that which is done on an individual basis will sometimes be instrumental in moving the child into the group and helping the group to value individuality at the same time.

An example that comes to mind is that of a child who was very much interested in nature and spent endless hours in the individual pursuit of collecting and mounting insects. When there was occasion for peers to see and learn about the efforts of this boy, their appreciation for individual effort was expanded; and some of them became interested in participating with the boy in the collection efforts. The boy was pleased about this; and, in effect, his individual activity moved him more solidly into a group of peers.

Let us go back for a moment to the story of John at the beginning of this chapter. This boy had problems, among which was the inability to read. He was living in a state of relative isolation from the community, from adults other than parents, and from peers. Through a process that involved many individuals, he moved in a relatively short time from isolation to a group participation that was most gratifying to him. In the beginning, he was involved in a relationship with individuals that enabled him to trust the adults with whom he was working and at the same time allowed him to risk himself in an area that had been very painful, his inability to read. From this individual work he moved into class participation and found satisfaction in this process, and this culminated in his performance as the narrator of the Christmas pageant.

Not all children will progress so rapidly because of their own peculiar makeup and personality characteristics and also because of the environment in which they find themselves. It is our job as recreators, teachers, physicians, social workers, psychologists, child-care personnel and so on to cultivate the attitudes and create the environment wherever possible to enable children to solve their problems so that they, too, can have a more positive view of themselves as individuals and as members of social groups.

In summary then, play and recreation serve many purposes for the development of the personality of the child. It is important to keep in mind the capacities of a child at a given developmental level so that adult standards for group participation are not pushed too early. This is especially true for children with emotional problems and even more so for children who are disturbed enough to require care in residential treatment centers. Some of these children are large physically, but they may have deficits in development. Thus, a strapping adolescent may need to move carefully and gradually from solitary to parallel and ultimately to group play, just as a young child does in its normal growth and development. If we are aware of this development ourselves, we can help the child move at a rate that is optimal for that child.

CHAPTER 10

Helping Children Find Their Past

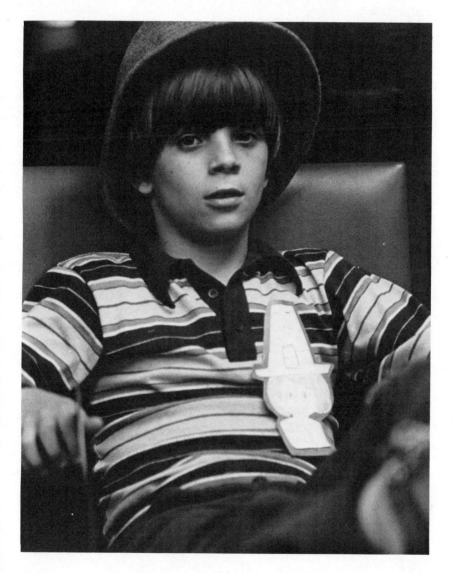

"I'd rather know than not know"

OF TIME AND PEOPLE

Busy tracing his past
  telephone calls, letters
  courthouse documents
  after fifteen years
  of here and there
  one day Jim asked,
  "I know it's important
  but why's it important
  to know about your kin?"

"It's like reading a road map
  if you know where you've been
  and where you are now
  it helps you to know
  where you want to go."

"Do you know your kinfolks?
  What're they like?" he said.
  "Tell me about your folks."

"One grandfather drove a wagon west
  the other was a banjo man
  great Uncle Fox
  was a gambling shark
  and Aunt Geneva
  was a Red Sox fan."

"Whatdoyouknow," Jim said,
  "they're just about like mine
  so far there's a preacher
  and a cattle thief
  some are bad
  and some are fine."

The search for our connections with the past goes on day after day for all of us. It may take the form of the free play of pleasant imagery in our memory banks, recalling scenes from earlier years as we go about our work and play. But it may also become the painful pursuit of fragments of the past floating uneasily on the screens of our minds, with occasional juxtaposition of useful and gratifying information. For some it may be the endless scanning of a barren field, hoping, searching for the appearance of something past that will add meaning to the present.

Apparently this search is a part of the human condition. The novel, *Roots*, by Alex Haley brought into sharp focus the idea of an ethnic group's need to know something of its own past. This is all the more dramatic when one considers the swiftness and completeness with which Africans were taken from their native habitat and transported to the New World as slaves, with no prospect of ever returning to the culture from which they had been traumatically torn. But individuals as well as groups have a need to know about their inheritance—who their parents, grandparents, and connections were, what they did, and where they did it. Countless literary works are concerned with this timeless search for an understanding of relationships with the past.

In this country there is a large population of children, quite apart from migrant families, who move from one place to another, never traveling the same route twice. These are the abandoned and the neglected children whose formative years are often spent in a succession of foster homes, children's homes, training schools, group homes, and treatment facilities.

Those of us who work with such children are especially cognizant of their yearnings for past connections. There is the preschool child who is suddenly moved from familiar surroundings, for many reasons, to live in a foster home. There is the latency-aged child who hangs on to fragmented memories of the past, often idealizing a father or mother who may have deserted or been found guilty of child neglect. Adolescents indulge in fantasies and construct plans, which they often execute, to find parents, siblings, or other relatives. By the time they reach adolescence, children are usually better able to recognize the realities of what may be found in the search, but this does not necessarily lessen the intensity with which they pursue the goal. Many say in different ways, "Whatever I find will be something worth knowing; even if it's a 'bad trip,' I'd rather know than not know." We are all familiar with the adolescent who searches for and finds a parent in distressed circumstances after the passage of many years. Even so, the knowing, though there is no possibility of reunion, seems to be enough to enable the adolescent to move ahead with his own future plans.

If knowledge of historical lines to the past is important for the development of the children's future, we should consider the ways in which the past can be preserved or rediscovered.

For younger children, foster parents or caseworkers may keep a running log or scrapbook complete with pictures of significant events in the child's life in a particular home. The scrapbook may contain pictures of important adults and children, pets, groups from school or neighborhood church, or whatever is familiar to the child. It should also contain serial pictures of the child's own growth and development.

This is the kind of record, whether formal or informal, that most sustaining families keep and to which children return in later years with much gratification. It is the kind of record keeping that some foster parents do intuitively. One foster mother, who cares for children for only a few weeks or months before they are placed indefinitely in another foster home or returned to their families, always makes a scrapbook with the child's name and picture on the front cover. Inside are recorded important dates, events, people, pets, and places. She has the child work on the scrapbook with her, and when the child is preparing to move on they review the book together. It then accompanies the child when he or she leaves. The children are fond of these scrapbooks and hold on to them as Linus holds onto his security blanket.

For the child who has moved six to a dozen times in a few years, there is often a lack of any continuity with the past—only a hazy parade of places and faces and a montage of fragmented memories, both good and bad. Children who have had few opportunities to keep in touch with their past but have begun to seek an identity of their own can make use of a historical search, which affords them a greater sense of control of their lives.

Henry, a latency-aged boy, used this kind of search. He had

many unanswered questions concerning his origins, and his therapist realized that the background history available was skimpy indeed. The options were to help him search out his beginnings or to indicate that nothing could be done and hope to divert his attention. After some lengthy discussions with his county social service worker, it was decided to help him uncover as much background material as could be located by a search of the records in his home county.

Henry and the social worker who participated in the search both contributed what they could to the effort. Information sought included the marriage of the mother and father, the birth of children, the parents' separation and divorce, foster home placements, school placements, court hearings, and current locations of family members when this could be ascertained. In order that the information located would be available to the boy and to others working with him, the information taken from the county records was recorded on tape cassettes for later playback. In addition, summary copies of the information were made for the boy, the social service worker, and his therapist at the agency where he was in residence. This system proved to be useful over a period of time in providing accurate background information for all to consider as the boy integrated information and asked further questions.

For James, another youngster, a study of a genealogical nature was in order because of the extraordinary number of family members who shifted irregularly in and out of his life. Because of his impulsive nature and some coping deficiencies in the area of social interaction, this youngster's talk of his family often confused those who worked with him. Part of this confusion was related to the fact that the youngster was basically a concrete thinker. As a result he did not, and could not, even use last names in identifying people he talked of.

With the help of the youngster and some family members, a family tree was developed, including great-grandparents, grandparents, parents, uncles, aunts, cousins, nephews, and nieces. This proved to be an invaluable aid to those working with the youngster in that it clarified, for all concerned, the former and present family relationships.

A chronological recording of placements, which included the

locations of various foster families and schools, was developed for a third youngster, Ted, to help him and others focus on where he had been at various times during his life. Developed over a span of time by Ted and his interning student therapist, the material included a graphic drawing which helped to make accurate awareness more likely. The method was most effective for this youngster because of the difficulty he had with reading. As a concrete visual learner, he used the available diagramming more successfully than he could ever use a written report or tape cassette.

Revelations of this kind can, however, be harmful if not handled therapeutically. For at least one latency-aged youngster, Charles, the information was too much to handle and, as a result, created problems for him and those working with him. Charles used denial and evasion to avoid the hurtful reality of the circumstances of his background, and coming to grips with this proved to be very uncomfortable for him. In turn, it was distressing for those working with him, as they suddenly had to deal with reactive behavior related to underlying hostility and anger.

It was later discovered that the information was inadvertently presented to the youngster in a situation that did not follow good therapeutic practice. Charles, who lived in a foster home, had not asked for information relative to his family prior to the time the information was shared. His brother, a resident in a children's treatment center, had benefited greatly from having such knowledge to work with, and the information was given to Charles during a talk with both youngsters. Charles, however, received no therapeutic support in dealing with the mass of information obtained. The result was great anxiety for the boy. The information evoked long-standing feelings of rejection and resultant hostility directed toward persons caring for him. The lesson to be learned by therapists and others is that we are dealing with powerful family dynamics when working with historical background material. It must be used sensitively and judiciously in alliance with the youngster.

Turning to older children, we can find other ways of helping them rediscover the past. Karl, for instance, had never seen his father, who had left the family a few days after the boy was born. He was the youngest of five children and the only boy. Karl remembered with anguish being told as a youngster by his mother and sisters that the father left home because he did not want a boy. At fifteen Karl did not believe this intellectually, but nevertheless he said, "I have to find out anyhow."

The mother, the only relative whose whereabouts he knew, could give no information as to the father's location; she did remember the name of a brother of the father and the town in which he had lived and worked in another state several years previously. With this meager information the boy's caseworker, after many telephone calls and letters, was finally able to trace the brother. He did not know where Karl's father was but knew the towns where some other members of the extended and widely scattered family lived. The caseworker was able to get in touch with several relatives but had no success in locating the father. This loosely connected and widely separated family still had some kind of network connection, however. A year and a half after the search began the caseworker received a telephone call from Karl's father in a distant state, expressing interest in his son. In the same week a letter arrived from one of the older sisters. On first hearing about these two inquiries, Karl sat quietly, tears flowing down his cheeks. After a long silence he said, "Well, it was worth waiting for; I guess somebody loves me."

Another boy, Bud, had lived with his mother for several years after his parents were divorced. These had been years of neglect, and antisocial behavior combined with sustained depression had brought him to a children's home. During his year and a half in residence he showed much improvement, but it was not thought advisable for him to return to live with either mother or father, as both were still in rather unsettled conditions.

During his time in psychotherapy he recalled many memories from early childhood of the extended family—uncles, aunts, and grandmother. He found their locations in other cities and states and made plans to visit each of them after leaving the children's home. Upon discharge, he lived with an older brother but followed through on his plans to visit the other family members. Several months after discharge Bud returned to the children's home for a visit, describing with great joy the feeling of belonging that this renewal of family ties had given him. "I no longer feel so alone as I once did" was his poignant way of describing the experience.

Jim's first twelve years had been spent in as many foster homes, and at fifteen he had been in a children's home for three years. During this stay he had made enormous progress. Although Jim had various relatives in the region, including his mother, none of them evidenced any interest in him, despite the efforts of his caseworker. Most of the relatives were unknown to Jim. An exception was his elderly maternal grandmother, who lived alone and had chronic medical problems. She was the one person in the family with whom Jim maintained a connection, paying an occasional brief visit and telephoning more frequently. It was through her that Jim learned of his father's death several states away. Although Jim could scarcely remember anything about his father, who had never been in touch with the boy during all these years, he said that he wished he could attend the funeral. The agency flew Jim and the housefather 800 miles to the airport closest to the town where the funeral was to be held. There they rented a car and drove to the small town to attend the funeral.

Later, in discussing this, Jim said, "I couldn't even remember him, so it didn't seem like my father's funeral." However, he commented that he had met many "nice" people on his father's side of the family, people he hadn't even known existed. It also seemed important to Jim that he had returned to his native state and the town where he was born. Also at the funeral was an older sister whom he had not seen in years, and this meant much to him. Within that same year an older brother, whom Jim had not seen since early childhood, shot himself. Again, he learned of this through the grandmother, and again he wanted to attend the funeral. This was in the region where the children's home was located, and Jim met many members of the extended family on the maternal side.

After this Jim became interested in recording information about the places he had lived, the family constellation, and the scattered members of his extended family. One day he remarked, "I guess most families have good people, bad people, and just plain crazy people, and mine sure has all of these."

The efforts involved in helping youngsters seek out roots, though difficult to quantify, pay dividends. Sometimes there is increased goal-directed movement to incorporate family ties. At other times there is an easier acceptance of the reality of the past with a freeing of energy for constructively facing the present and the future. The youngster needs to accept the root beginnings for what they are—links with the past, heritage connections to be honored and to be put into proper perspective.

After the Children Leave

*What had happened to their friends
who have gone?*

WITH LOVE

We walked along the sand
in her fishing village
walking, talking, and watching
the oystermen come home
while she asked questions
one on top another
is Angie still there
when will she go home
have they found a place
for Todd when he goes
what about Mr. Fowlkes
and Ms. Biggers and Sue
and all the others
then I miss you too

While she talked she told
of how it was at home
he doesn't drink so much
and mama's happier too
at school they like
the way I'm learning
and not being bad
so much the way I was

Now and then she'd bend
to gather a pretty shell
assigning it by name
for some distant friend
and filling to the brim
my pockets heavy with love

Historically, children's homes have been just that: a place where children could live if necessary until they were ready to go out into the world. For many this meant late adolescence or early adulthood. Staff members in these institutions were in fact parent surrogates and could lend support through many years, and the staff was probably less mobile, in most instances, than staff members in children's group homes and residential centers are today.

In many locations, these living circumstances have changed. New treatment programs have been developed, and many former children's homes and orphanages have been converted to treatment programs. As a result, the stay of troubled children is limited in time from a few months to two or three years at most.

There remains a critical problem for many children—the neglected, unwanted, and abandoned with marked emotional problems—namely, where they will live following time in a treatment facility. A partial solution for some may be the establishment by the treatment programs of satellite group homes where treatment support services can be provided if needed for longer periods of time. This kind of continuity of care requires much coordinated effort among social service bureaus, which have usually been awarded legal custody of these children by the courts, and the treatment facility and its satellite group homes.

This is a much-needed service but one that most treatment programs are not in a position to provide. When a satellite group home is possible, it does enable rootless children to grow up in a relatively stable environment with a greater potential for unsevered and extended attachments, a continuing problem in this nomadic segment of the child population. Because of combinations of factors, such as abandonment and the severity, intensity, and chronicity of problems, posttreatment placement is a serious consideration.

Although one wishes that all children might have a warm, nurturing, natural family in which to grow up, this is certainly not the reality. After residential care and treatment, many will return to their own families, but others will go to relatives, foster homes, and a variety of group homes, children's homes, and extended-care institutions.

Wherever they go, other forms of professional attention, perhaps less intense than residential treatment, often are needed.

There are many ways in which the treatment facility where the child has lived can be of great help in the transition to another placement. This follow-up or after-care is extremely important, and yet it is an area that is still much neglected. Many retrospective studies have been made of what happens to these children— and these are of value—but there are too few programs with a follow-up plan in which the children are seen at regular intervals after discharge.

The time after discharge to home community is critical in the life of the child and the family. Planned after-care can (1) benefit the child directly; (2) aid parents in their relationship with the child; (3) provide consultation for community-based agencies concerned with the welfare of the child. If such a plan is possible, it adds immeasurably to the continuity of care we all desire but so infrequently bring about. In addition, follow-up has become increasingly important in that funding sources for children's programs are inquiring more searchingly into what happens after discharge. They want to know the effectiveness of the programs for which funds are being solicited.

Follow-up also offers instruction and refinement of skills to those providing residential care. Through follow-up, a staff learns better what it is doing, or in some instances, not doing.

Follow-up plans have to be devised for a particular program, as each treatment program is unique. One successful plan will be described in detail; then, several other possible approaches will be mentioned. Each could be modified, or elements could be combined for a specific program.

A SUCCESSFUL FOLLOW-UP PROGRAM

A children's treatment center three years in operation was fortunate to receive a five-year grant through the National Institute for Mental Health for a Children's Center Field Unit. These funds were sufficient to employ an additional child psychiatrist, a psychiatric social worker, two special education teachers, and a secretary.

The goals of the field unit were as follows:

Primary
1. Direct follow-up care of discharged children
2. Case consultation in the communities
3. Preadmission screening of prospective admissions
Secondary
1. Professional education in the communities
2. Community education for citizen groups
3. Staff education for
   a. Children's treatment center staff
   b. Trainees in various programs at the center (general and child psychiatry residents, pediatric residents, social-work students, psychology interns, recreation interns, education students, nursing students, and occupational therapy interns)
4. Research

Organization of the Field Unit

For those children and families in the metropolitan area of the children's center, follow-up care was possible through the regular activities of the Child-Adolescent Clinic, which was an integral part of the operation. However, children were admitted to the center from the entire state, and those from more distant areas were the focus of the field unit's work.

With the additional personnel employed through grant funds, three traveling teams were mobilized initially from the total staff. Each was to visit its area once a month. In the far western part of the state the base of operations was a public health clinic located in a small town. In the central part of the state the base was a joint social service–public health clinic center. The third team was based in the outpatient department of a pediatric hospital located in a large metropolitan area in the eastern part of the state. The teams spent two days each month at these sites.

Thus there were initially four places approximately 125 miles apart where follow-up services could take place. These sites had been selected because of the clustering of referrals and admissions from these areas since the children's psychiatric center opened. There were referrals from other parts of the state too, but they were scattered. Periodically a "roving" team was organized to follow these more isolated cases.

At first the traveling teams were comprised of a child psychiatrist, psychologist, social worker, nurse, and teacher, all senior staff members. Later, as experience was gained, the composition and number on a given team were altered as events demanded. The plan was for every professional staff person to participate in the field unit activities. On occasion child-care persons were included also, but problems in scheduling for these persons, who worked rotating shifts, made their participation less frequent than was desirable. On a given trip many activities other than follow-up took place, but the follow-up activity is highlighted in this description.

The Field Unit Follow-Up Plan

The field unit secretary coordinated all activities from her office at the children's center. She was in telephone and letter communication with each base of operation during the interval between visits. The personnel in the agencies where the follow-up visits took place were primarily responsible for coordinating appointments for discharged children and their parents. These follow-up visits for each discharged child were scheduled monthly at first, and if progress was satisfactory the interval was increased to two, three, and six-months and ultimately to one year. In other words, frequency of visits depended on needs.

The willingness of parents, on all socioeconomic levels, to participate in this plan was probably related to early preparation while the child was in the treatment center. The importance of follow-up was explained and participation requested of parents (or parent surrogates) and was made part of the final discharge plan. In the five years of field unit operation, only one parent stated that she wanted no future contact with any representative of the children's center. Her child had made excellent progress in a short time but was removed from the program against clinical advice for reasons known only to the mother. Her wish was respected, although unsolicited information came informally from the child's teacher.

Some parents lived over 300 miles from the children's center, and frequent visits to the center were often difficult or impossible. The field unit served as a valuable bridge in these instances by carrying letters, drawings by the child, photographs of the child, or cassette tapes of the child's voice; and in several cases portable videotape recordings were used to show the parents sound and action pictures of their child in activities at the center. These procedures were reversed to keep the child's family associations as fresh as possible. Such selected maneuvers were important connections between child and family in many instances.

Continued involvement with parents and community referral sources during the child's stay at the center created an alliance that made the child's reentry into the family and community much easier. In some cases, if several community agencies were involved, an interim meeting was held, with all present, at the field unit's base. After-care planning thus became a joint endeavor, utilizing the active participation of all concerned.

If, for some reason, a predischarge meeting with involved agencies could not be arranged at the field unit base, a team representative visited the different agency offices to keep them up to date on the child's progress. Thus, a child's return to the community was an informed, coordinated event.

Such direct visits were of particular value in relation to schools. A teacher from the center would go to the school from which the student had come for a prearranged meeting with principal, teacher, and school guidance counselor. The child's academic progress and behavioral characteristics would be discussed. Incidentally, the children in the residential program, from whatever region in the state, used the textbooks of the school system from which they had come.

In some cases, especially for children with specific learning disabilities, a videotape was made at the center demonstrating the child's particular learning style and the teaching methods used there. This method was also used to demonstrate any special techniques of behavior management the center-based teachers had found useful for that child. Such efforts were well received and went far in helping the local school to be prepared for the return of a child who may have caused widespread consternation and disruption before being referred for residential treatment. Often, the school's expectations were markedly altered from negative to positive.

The follow-up field trips were anticipated with enthusiasm by staff, discharged children, and community agencies alike. Most of the children had stayed in the center from four to five months to a year (none longer by regulation) and had formed attachments to the place and the people. They eagerly inquired about staff and other children. Through regular visits, a level of rapport was built up between the children's residential program and community agencies, which is of utmost importance for successful treatment of disturbed children.

Although the direct child visits and the case consultations probably were most important in developing the level of cooperation among parents, agencies, and the residential center, many other activities involving large numbers of persons and agencies with center staff were of considerable importance in creating awareness of and support for children's services in general.

Over the years the field unit activities were modified depending on community needs. For example, some of the more distant communities developed regional mental health clinics, and such close involvement of children's center staff became less necessary. Other areas requesting services became field sites for similar work. Professional groups, including mental health clinics, requested continuing workshops on children's disorders and treatment approaches.

After each field unit visit, whether in an established site or on one of the "roving" tours, brief information about each child visited was posted on a large bulletin board at the center so that the staff could know what happened to each child. Not all children went home, of course. Some went to foster homes and group homes, some to boarding schools, and a few to indefinite-stay units in the state hospital system. The follow-up covered these children too. The staff knew who was doing well, who not so well, and where every child was located except for the few who moved in the five-year-period to other states. Detailed information on the status of each child was duly recorded in special files, thus providing a rich resource for clinical research by staff members of all disciplines.

Finally, the continuing statewide involvement of staff—who came from many sections of this country and from other countries—was a valuable adjunct in a most important aspect of work with disturbed children, that is, an appreciation and understanding of the sociocultural context within which the child lives.

Even though the task of follow-up was an arduous one, it proved helpful to many children, their families, and community agencies. At the same time it was most instructive to staff members and to hundreds of students over the years. Moreover, it had its pleasurable and rejuvenating aspects for a busy staff—quiet drives through picturesque valleys, panoramic mountain roads with sweeping vistas, lodging and delicious meals in a hundred-year-old inn in a quaint old town, or a clambake in a fishing village at sunset by the ocean.

It was a busy, productive time for the total staff. When the five-year federal funds were no longer available, the state was pleased enough with the results that the legislature appropriated funds to continue the work. Nearly twenty years have passed since the field units were first established, and they are still in operation.

SUGGESTIONS FOR POSSIBLE FOLLOW-UP PLANS

The follow-up experience described above is unusual in many ways, and it is not possible in most residential programs. The field unit plan took place in an institution that was a joint venture of the state Department of Mental Health and a state-supported medical school. There were forty inpatient beds, a day-care program, a child-adolescent outpatient clinic, and a pediatric liaison service. At the time there was no other approved training program in child psychiatry in that state, and mental health clinics were widely separated.

Under these conditions, this children's residential center was mandated by statute to proceed in every way possible to improve care and treatment of disturbed children in the state. At the same time attention was to be directed to preventive aspects in treating mental and emotional disturbance. There was support from the state legislature, the Department of Mental Health, and the medical school, as well as some support from federal funding sources.

The program was established a few years before the federal funding for mental health programs that resulted from the report of the President's Commission on Mental Health and Illness in the early sixties. Funding for the first five years of the field unit did come from federal sources, however. Such funds are scarcer now, and residential programs have multiplied throughout the country. How then without large expenditures are we to accomplish follow-up in a manner helpful to children and at the same time informative to those who operate residential treatment centers and children's homes?

The following ideas may be helpful in considering follow-up plans.

Geographic Area

In the plan described earlier, in which children came from throughout the state, a large map of the state was mounted on a wall. The pins were coded, so that green, for example, represented one child and red represented five children from a given town or county. Thus, at a glance, one had a graphic view of the clustering of admissions from a particular place. Among other uses, this visible display gave some rough idea of sites for location of field bases and the personnel needed.

Use of Outpatient Services

Many children's homes and residential centers do not have clearly identifiable outpatient services. The work done with families while the child is in residence is a form of outpatient service, as is the intake and screening service through which a child enters the program. It is regrettable that many residential centers end their planned service with discharge. It is as though the child were kept in residence until "fixed," and it is rare that a child's problems are "fixed" in such a delineated time frame. Why not create a special outpatient (or follow-up) program? This would not have to be an outpatient clinic in the usual sense, as many residential programs are hard pressed to staff the primary program and could not staff an open clinic. But it might be possible to set aside a regular day each month when some of the clinical staff might devote time to outpatient appointments for discharged children, the frequency of visits to be established for each child. Many programs now serve more restricted geographic areas; thus, many families are within commuting distance, and return presents fewer problems.

The eagerness with which children return, even for short visits, to a residential center is impressive. They want to renew acquaintance with staff and other children. They are especially concerned with what has happened to other children who may have left since they did. Sometimes it is possible to honor a child's request to "bring Billy [or Jane] back on the day that I come." In addition, the return of children to the residential campus is of value to those children in residence. These children always wonder, inquire, and really want to know what has happened to their friends who are now outside the program. Return visits are reassuring to those still in residence and often serve as a stimulus to some children to "work on my problems so I can go home like John did."

A Field Team

Many children admitted to a residential center are for various reasons (mainly distance and travel funds) unable to return at scheduled intervals for follow-up. This can preclude any case consultation with parents, parent surrogates, or agency. These consultative services are invaluable in the management plan for the early months after discharge and are a most reassuring service for the residential center to offer.

Providing for a traveling team or individual from existing staff to make periodic tours to gather postdischarge information need not necessarily require a great amount of time or money. A possible schedule might be at one, three, six, and twelve months after discharge. Of course, the direct or consultative service would be minimal under these circumstances. But even so, the individual or team in many instances could be helpful in directing child and family to other services should they appear to be needed.

Telephone or Letter Follow-Up

Following up by telephone or letter may be the least desirable alternative, but it has certain merits. Again, a predetermined schedule for collecting information must be arranged, and the responsibility must be clearly delineated. Otherwise, in the all-consuming urgency of residential care, activities that seem less critical often go undone.

Information gathered in this way should be posted regularly on a special bulletin board for all staff members to see. Then, when children inquire about other children no longer in the program, they can be given definite information. If things are not going well for a particular discharged child, the inquiring child can be given specific information rather than "I don't know," or "We haven't heard." The child can be told what further efforts are being made to help the other child. Children handle this kind of exchange better than the uncertainty of not knowing. It is reassuring to them to know that "helping" does not begin and end with the significant adults now present in their lives.

Information to Seek

Getting information in follow-up care can be quite simple, or it can be as complex as one wishes to make it. In fact, the whole endeavor can become a highly sophisticated research effort. Most programs, however, especially smaller ones and those without strong academic (university or medical school) connections, will find it difficult to develop extensive and expensive research efforts.

Certain kinds of information are helpful in assessing the current functioning of a child:

1. The child's relation to self—for example, any marked degree of depression, the child's handling of anxiety, and his sense of self-esteem

2. The child's relationship to family, foster family, group home; how the child views these relationships, how parents view them, and how other family or group members view them

3. The child's relationship with the community, including academic and behavioral adaptation to school and functioning in other community activities such as Scouts, playground, church, or any part of the community arena in which the child moves

4. The current behavioral characteristics of the child—the quantity and quality of persisting behaviors that were instrumental in admission to residential treatment or group care in the first place. This kind of information gives some basis for comparison of the child's current adjustment with that of the past. A checklist for all these areas might be devised by staff members.

SUPPORT FOR FOLLOW-UP

Obviously the amount of monetary expenditure for follow-up will vary according to the many factors already mentioned. Probably the simplest form of follow-up could be managed even by small programs with minimal strain on the budget.

However, there are other, even more basic considerations of prime importance to the success of a follow-up program. The director and board of directors must see value in and give full support to a plan if it is to succeed. The families, parent surrogates, or agencies must understand the reasons for follow-up and must be reassured that it will not be instrusive and will not be done in a manner that will invade their privacy. For these conditions to exist, the follow-up plan must be part of the total program explained in the intake and admission process. Because of the rapport that is usually established and solidified between a residential agency and families while a child is in residence, this is not likely to pose a problem. With gradual accommodation to the idea, most parents will see follow-up for what it is, a continuity of care that can be most helpful to them and their child as well as to staff and the children still remaining in residential treatment and care.

Anyone who has seen staff and children crowd around a follow-up bulletin board for news about children who have been in residence and are now "out there somewhere," or who has fielded the questions discharged children ask about their friends "at the center," knows the importance of follow-up. If one has not had this experience, it is something to anticipate, for no residential program is complete without follow-up.

CHAPTER 12

Experiences in Verse

Go, my friend, for it is time

DEAR MOMMIE, DEAR DADDY

I was there on the day
they brought them in
Regina, Bill, and Chip
all were frantic lost

At first a chorus of tears
where was mommie and why
daddy was already gone away
later when the tears slowed

they noticed the Dictaphone
what did it do
could they write a letter
each of them please

They did—8, 6, and 4
dear mommie dear daddy
I love you I love you
all the same—8, 6, and 4

They didn't know still don't
the reason they were there
mommie had made a final plan
first the children then herself

DREAMS

Langston Hughes soared
High into the vaulted blue
In my view
When he wrote:
"Hold fast to dreams
For if dreams should die,
Life is a broken winged bird
That cannot fly."

You are so young
Lying there, battered,
That I ponder, wonder
Where do dreams begin?

Do you have dreams?
How could so young
A neophyte network
Of neural strands
Support dreams
Of any kind?

Perhaps your dreams
Are not cognitive
At all (or need not be).
Maybe they're only
The chemical yearnings
Of naked receptors
Lying unanswered
In a broken world.

GOODNIGHT

When you slammed the car door
cutting four-stitches worth
in Carl's middle finger
the night was darker for you

Building on years of experience
at being blamed for things
falls, cuts, broken vases
tricycle wrecks, dirty faces

You expected your world to teeter
but Carl didn't blame you at all
for anyone could plainly see
the hurt that covered your face

Later, after stitches, we talked
all together; you cried like a baby
from sorrow for Carl, relief for self
that there was another ending

At ten that night my phone rang
your voice was calm and clear.
"Goodnight, we're both all right,"
was all you said, "Goodnight."

SINGING COCKLES

She was a wild thing
Fourteen
Long, black hair
Blue eyes and see-through skin

Long nights of running amok
In the remote mountains
To be found chilled
Starved, insect-eaten, and gone

She cut her wrists
Severed some tendons
Clawed her skin
Battered her head
Chewed a Gillette Blue-Blade
Drank a wino's Strawberry Farms
Down in the Fan where she ran

But before she left
To return to her mountains
She sang haunting ballads

Passed along
Through generations
I can still hear her singing
"She wheeled a wheelbarrow
Through streets broad and narrow—

And now she's married
Married a young man
A good man the neighbors said
Who owned a small goat farm

They have a baby girl
And the Public Health Nurse
Who keeps up with things
Brings a message now and then

The nurse sees her rocking
On the front porch
Holding her baby
And hears her
"Singing cockles and mussels
Alive, Alive-O."

ONE WAY ONLY

Even though I think
That I understand
Partially at least
The origins of your hurts
Deprivations by many names
In many places
For many years

It is no less frightening
To see you mobilizing
Every ounce of energy
To destroy the foes
Those past and yet to come
Some real as day and night
Some synthesized in twilight
By your inevitable-end
One-product brain

I sit and search for the presence
Of one single adult
Who may be someone special
But so far all I find
Are shreds of many persons
Dumped indiscriminately
Into the hopper of your mind

MOVING ON

A year ago when we talked
you raved of space encroachments
running away, tandem injustices
destruction, and what the hell

Today we talk of other things
semester's exams completed
how you think you did in math
the training schedule for track

A joke that someone told you
a girl you've got an eye on
another kid's troubling troubles
of things yet to be

You've moved on, far on
this eventful year
from an uncertain, nowhere kid
who had no room for laughter

To one whose tightened joints
move ball-and-socket smooth
whose spirited voice tells
how you embrace this time and place

Now the older girls chase you
still chaste, but not in mind
down these ever-shortening
long halls of innocence

OLD FRIENDS

We had known each other for years
Frequent encounters in several agencies
From the time he was a wild-animal pup
To the present, a pretty civil young man

One day recently he said to me
"I've no family at all anymore
So you're my oldest and best friend
And I'm glad."

That made the long advocacy worth it
For I knew now that he had many friends
He surely was right on the first count
And I'm glad to accept the second

THE PARTING

Kenny was looking dapper
Ready to leave for the airport
For the flight home
After a year and a month

He knocked at my door
To say goodbye
A little glad, a little sad
He'd write he said

"I've been with a lot of kids here,
And I'm not afraid anymore."
He gathered his gifts together
And went slowly—glad and sad

GOODBYE

That crayon picture you made,
A racer, rocket powered,
Thrusting, gone,
Hangs where you put it
On my wall that day
Before you left that night.
It says "Goodbye, (signed) Dan."
Today I wonder where you are.
Somewhere safe, I trust,
With motor
Idling.

FAREWELL

Go, my friend,
For it is time.
I shall miss you
Each day.

We have been here
These many months
Together,
Learning.

Now you know what I know.
No truths to sermonize
You will discover it yourself
In unsuspecting moments ahead.

Index

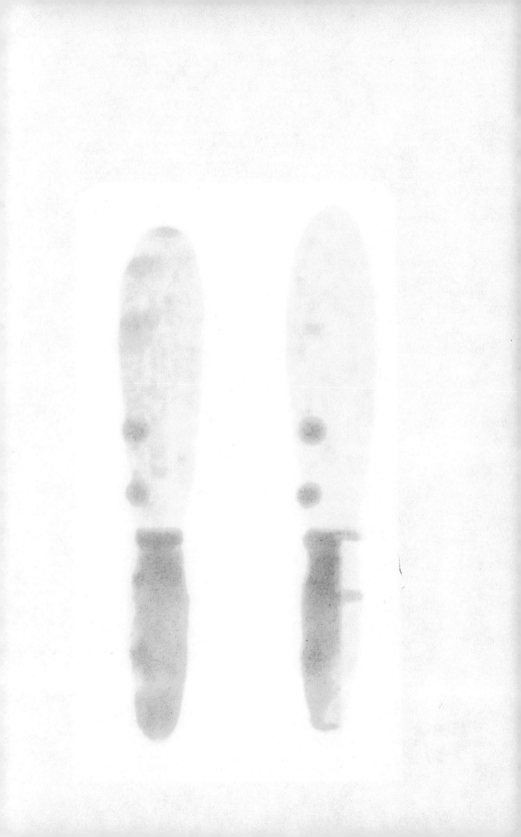